In Search of Godzilla

In Search of Godzilla

Myth, Stagecraft and Politics in Ishiro Honda's Masterpiece

RICK WALLACH

McFarland & Company, Inc., Publishers
Jefferson, North Carolina

LIBRARY OF CONGRESS CATALOGING-IN-PUBLICATION DATA

Names: Wallach, Rick author
Title: In search of Godzilla : myth, stagecraft and politics in Ishiro Honda's masterpiece / Rick Wallach.
Description: Jefferson, North Carolina : McFarland & Company, Inc., Publishers, 2025. | Includes bibliographical references and index.
Identifiers: LCCN 2025024191 | ISBN 9781476697826 paperback ∞
    ISBN 9781476656137 ebook
Subjects: LCSH: Gojira (Motion picture) | BISAC: PERFORMING ARTS / Film / Genres / Science Fiction & Fantasy | LCGFT: Film criticism
Classification: LCC PN1995.9.G63 W35 2025 | DDC 791.43/72—dc23/eng/20250604
LC record available at https://lccn.loc.gov/2025024191

ISBN (print) 978-1-4766-9782-6
ISBN (ebook) 978-1-4766-5613-7

© 2025 Rick Wallach. All rights reserved

No part of this book may be reproduced or transmitted in any form or by any means, electronic or mechanical, including photocopying or recording, or by any information storage and retrieval system, without permission in writing from the publisher.

Front cover image from Adobe Firefly

Printed in the United States of America

McFarland & Company, Inc., Publishers
  Box 611, Jefferson, North Carolina 28640
    www.mcfarlandpub.com

In memory of Billy Wallach,
who took his four-year-old son
to the American Museum of Natural History
to meet the dinosaurs,
then took his six-year-old son
to the movies to meet Godzilla.

Acknowledgments

I WISH TO THANK ALL THOSE RESEARCHERS and writers who had the perspicacity to take Godzilla seriously, and whose work has been of immeasurable assistance to this author: Chon Noriega, Stuart Galbraith IV, Donald Ritchie, Michael J. Blouin, William Tsutsui, Peter H. Brothers, David Kalat, Mark Hayden, Brian Solomon, August Ragone, Steve Ryfle, and the editors of *Life* Magazine. If I've neglected to mention anyone here, my apologies. You'll find yourselves in the bibliography.

I also want to thank my friend and colleague of four decades, Peter Josyph, for badgering me into undertaking this richly rewarding project; Matthew Aucheau for his sensitive reading and commentary on an early draft; Terra Kirkland for reminding me to discuss Godzilla's efficacy as an instigator of nightmares; and Darrell Arnold, editor of *Humanities and Technology Review*. Most of all, I want to thank my warrior princess, Rowena, for taking care of the domestic challenges, and me, so I could work on this book with a clear head.

Contents

Acknowledgments	vi
Prologue: Monsters and Mythopoesis	1
I. The Growth of Critical Response	15
II. A Tale of Two Directors	24
III. Dramatis Personae	37
IV. An American *Benshi* in Tokyo: Steve Martin	66
V. The Atomic Genie	70
VI. The Mythic and Religious Gojira	76
VII. Visual Poetics: *Gojira* as Ritual and Noh Performance	96
VIII. Godzilla Ecology	104
IX. The Science Fiction Rhetoric of *Gojira*	122
X. *Shin Gojira:* Parody, Politics and Commentary	133
XI. Another Postscript: *Godzilla Minus One*	147
Epilogue	155
References	157
Index	163

"Civilization is the ultimate destiny of the Culture.... Civilizations are the most external and artificial states of which a species of developed humanity is capable. They are a conclusion, the thing-become succeeding the thing-becoming, death following life, rigidity following expansion ... petrifying world-city following mother-earth and the spiritual childhood."
—Oswald Spengler, *The Decline of the West*

Prologue

Monsters and Mythopoesis

WE NEED TO BE OF SEVERAL minds when considering representations of Godzilla, whether it is the 1954 Japanese original film, *Gojira*, or Transworld's redacted 1956 American release, *Godzilla, King of the Monsters*. During the past few decades appreciation of director Ishiro Honda's masterwork has grown exponentially. Full of political, social, historical, and even religious commentary, it has become the subject of critical discussion, from the most rudimentary viewer responses to sophisticated poststructural and postcolonial studies. Although it was received originally as kitsch, decades of critical second and third considerations have revealed it to be a complex overlay of visual and auditory texts, a hall of mirrors enhanced by a remarkable musical score and ambient sound.

The story of the circumstances which culminated in the original 1954 film is a very long one. Most accounts of where Godzilla as cinematic icon originated begin with the Pacific War, especially with Hiroshima and Nagasaki. But that's an abbreviated version. The monster's roots actually go down into Japanese myth, the whaling fields of the Marshall Islands, and into African and Indonesian soil as far back as the late nineteenth century, and into Chinese folklore thousands of years old.

My personal fascination with this dark, sad movie began two years before I ever saw it, in a museum gallery in New York City where, although I couldn't know it at the time, the story of Godzilla had received its initial impetus, too. In the summer of 1954 the American Museum of Natural History was a very different place. Its exterior hasn't changed much, an edifice of granitic blocks reveling in their cruel weight. The big changes to it, tracking advances in the biological sciences, microscopy, paleontology, and architectural fashion,

Prologue: Monsters and Mythopoesis

would happen inside. Splendid old galleries, the museum's catacombs clustered around a few high-ceilinged lobbies and rotundas. Hallways between them felt too high and narrow, and many of the galleries were claustrophobic. Stone staircases linking the floors splayed at their landings like river deltas while crazed windows at the ends of its corridors dimmed the urban light filtering in from the streets.

In the Hall of Reptiles I met my prequel to the dinosaurs: two enormous Komodo dragons mounted in a glass diorama, one maintaining vigilance while the other bit into a boar it had killed or scavenged. These charcoal-colored monsters were brought to the museum in 1926 by a globe-trotting socialite-explorer named W. Douglas Burden with the encouragement and support of the museum's director, Henry Fairfield Osborn. Burden had read of the capture of a few specimens prior to World War I by the Dutch colonial museum of the East Indies (Burden 16–17), but with records of that episode scattered by war he resolved to travel to the Lesser Sunda Islands and secure specimens for the museum in New York.

A few years after my first museum visit I would read Burden's journal of his expedition to what were then called the Dutch East Indies in a facsimile edition of *National Geographic*. Ironically, the prehistoric world brooded over the expedition. En route to Indonesia through China in 1923 Burden and his wife encountered an old friend and another Museum of Natural History–sponsored explorer, paleontologist Roy Chapman Andrews. Temporarily trapped in a luxury hostel in Peking during the Zhili-Fengtian conflict, Andrews told Burden of his discoveries of the fossilized nest of the Oviraptor (which he mistakenly believed to be Protoceratops). He was the first to prove that dinosaurs laid eggs.* Further inspired by Andrews' achievements, Burden negotiated his way out of the besieged city and continued to the Lesser Sundas and his date with his dragons. Later that year Andrews would bring his dinosaur eggs back to the Museum in New York.

Decades further on I would read about how Burden's celebrity inspired the envy of his friend, another adventuring socialite, documentary filmmaker Merian C. Cooper. Cooper's plan to make a film of his friend's pursuit of the legendary dragons of Komodo on their island redoubt was, however, waylaid by a dream. The developmental pathway

---

* Although he was unable to determine which came first.

Prologue: Monsters and Mythopoesis

from these prehistoric survivals to Godzilla would wind through that dream, elliptically but surely.* Meanwhile, I had my own dreams, terrifying dreams, waiting for me just down the hall.

Turning through vaulted entryways into lofty rooms, also dimly lit, burnished skeletons of monsters confronted me. These galleries exhibiting prehistoric death—for the animatronic era was not yet upon us—were, like the vanished world they represented, foreboding places. In the center of the Jurassic Hall an Allosaurus bent over its Brontosaurus dinner radiating gratification despite its fleshlessness. Around another corner and through another time tunnel the Cretaceous Hall featured an old-school *Tyrannosaurus rex* skeleton towering into the murk, tail dragging behind, tiny two-fingered hands raised in a saurian *mudra*, head askance as though catching something out of the corner of its eye. A child needed to lean slightly backwards to take in its full height. At four years old, "extinction" didn't mean enough to me to ameliorate a shiver of dread. A floor-level glass case displayed a life-sized replica Tyrannosaurus skull, enabling a child to meet his bad dream nose to nose as though my Komodo dragons had burgeoned in size and horror by a factor of ten.

In both halls dust whirled in light slanting through dirty windows into near gloom, imparting a strobic effect to those gorgons posed as though yet pursuing their hungry affairs. Murals depicted these revenants *in situ*, in cycad fringed swamps surrounded with tree ferns, or striding across volcano-rimmed prairies. One mural was of that same Allosaurus, here fully fleshed, leaning over its quarry tugging bolts of meat towards its mouth with its claws. These were the paintings of Charles R. Knight, whose representations of prehistoric life dominated the imagination of generations of spectators. His Brontosaurus, a dun olive giant wallowing in a lake, gazing over its shoulder, was our archetypal sauropod for much of a century. Knight's faceoff between Tyrannosaurus and Triceratops approaching one another across a prairie, each with dreadful confidence, personified the implacability of ancient life. For my generation, as for those who came before and immediately after, the way Knight envisioned dinosaurs was the way they *were*.

His representations heavily influenced stop-motion animation

---

* See Mark Cotta Vaz, *Living Dangerously: The Adventures of Merian C. Cooper, Creator of* King Kong (New York: Villard, 2005).

Prologue: Monsters and Mythopoesis

wizards Willis O'Brien and Ray Harryhausen to re-create his dinosaurs in movies like *The Lost World, King Kong* and *The Valley of Gwangi* (Fradken). A young Mexican-American artist named Marcel Delgado fabricated remarkably accurate, adjustable sculptures of Knight's beasts for these pioneer animators to bring to life. In a real if, again, elliptical sense, they ultimately influenced the form Godzilla's creators, who so admired those two pioneers of stop motion animation, would give him. Knight himself had revised the forms those beasts had been given by the feuding paleontologists of the *fin de siècle*, Othniel Marsh and Edwin Drinker Cope, and by the earlier misconceptions, in 1854, of Richard Owen and Benjamin Waterhouse Hawkins' dinosaur sculptures in the Crystal Palace exhibition in London. The hugely influential museum artist laid to rest in the popular imagination the competing representations of their discoveries.

Cope and Marsh's battles over fossil fields and funding, as vicious as any one-on-one between those departed leviathans themselves, had yielded their fury to history and anecdote. So had Hawkins' and Owen's quadruped Iguanodons, which oddly resembled the living dragons of Indonesia whose discovery was 70 years in the future. Over the coming decades other paleontologists would proffer their own amendments, ever aware of our resistance. Feathers or bright colors on dinosaurs? Those dragging tails replaced by balance beams? We surrendered our faith in Knight's depictions no more readily than we abandoned the pretty poetry of Genesis.

In April 1956 *Godzilla, King of the Monsters* opened in the U.S. and dominated the summer popcorn season. With an irony I would not appreciate for decades, it followed one of the year's previous blockbusters, John Huston's film of *Moby Dick*. On my insistence, because I had read the Classics Illustrated comic book versions of Melville's saga, my father took me to see it sometime during the winter. Unbeknownst to me, as to most Americans, the Japanese name of Godzilla, *Gojira*, was a conflation of *gorira*, the Japanese loan word for "gorilla," with *kujira*, for "whale."

Following the American release of the original Japanese version on DVD in 2006 by Classic Media, it became common knowledge the gorilla who inspired the first syllable of this portmanteau was *King Kong*. The 20th anniversary re-release of Merian C. Cooper's 1933 classic reaped a box office windfall in Japan. It had been Cooper's original

Prologue: Monsters and Mythopoesis

idea to make a film about a rampaging gorilla battling one of his friend Douglas Burden's Komodo dragons.

Meanwhile, gorillas, which had only been discovered in the mid-nineteenth century, were beginning to show up as taxidermies in European museum collections but live captures remained rarities. News reports about Alfred the gorilla, a captive in the Bristol Zoo in England, became widespread in the 1930s. Cooper reportedly had a dream about a giant gorilla, likely inspired by Alfred's currency and popularity, which inspired him to switch out Burden's dragons altogether for a giant ape, rendering his film about an expedition to a mysterious South Pacific island uniquely his own. In the course of scripting his film those discarded Komodo dragons became an allosaurus and other ultimate Lazarus taxons worthy of combat with Cooper's giant ape.

The cinematic environment which spalded *Gojira* and his American redaction was rich, fertile, and complex. The 1953 American monster movie *The Beast from 20,000 Fathoms* was also recording worldwide box-office success before arriving in Japan, a fact of which the Toho Studios brass were well aware. Extrapolated from a Ray Bradbury short story, "The Fog Horn," it grossed nearly $5,000,000 in the U.S. alone. Then, in December of 1954, the Walt Disney production of Jules Verne's 1870 science-fantasy novel *20,000 Leagues Under the Sea* was released. It grossed $17,440,000 in the U.S., fueled no doubt by ubiquitous promotions on the Walt Disney television show where I first watched it. Like *Gojira*, Verne's tale was underpinned by a sense of political disillusionment.

As Honda's film engaged the shock and bitterness of the loss of the Pacific War, the French work, with its mysterious ship-wrecking mechanical "sea monster," resonated with disappointment at the squandered promises of the revolutions of 1848 and the Polish revolution of 1863. Perhaps not as ironic as it might seem, the frigate carrying Professor Pierre Aronnax—a marine biologist and one of several precursors of *Gojira*'s Professor Yamane—is attacked by Captain Nemo's submarine *Nautilus* near Japan. What's more, the iconic battle between the crew of the *Nautilus* and a giant squid in the original French novel, which had been translated into Japanese years earlier by Yu Ishikawa, seemed to impact producer Tomoyuki Tanaka and author Shigeru Kayama's first treatment for *Gojira*. With the cumbersome early title "The Giant Monster from 20 Million Miles Beneath the Sea," Gojira was conceived as a

5

Prologue: Monsters and Mythopoesis

giant cephalopod, but re-framed as a dinosaur in short order. And there was that talismanic "twenty" again.

In any event, the box office achievements of the three films encouraged Toho to risk an unheard of investment in a monster movie, $900,000 (the equivalent of $8.5 million today). It sounds like a pittance compared to contemporary film budgets but in a time of limited resources it was enough to put the studio in financial jeopardy. Such was *Kong*'s box office influence. Such, too, was the novel pressure of television, a recently introduced home entertainment medium with which cinema now had to compete (Brothers, *Mushroom Clouds and Mushroom Men* 5).

However, the source of the concluding pair of syllables of our monster's name, *-jira*, was less often speculated, aside from the beast being huge and a marine organism. Along with a couple of other, likely apocryphal, attributions the best known origin fable was Tanaka's contention that the monster was named after a hulking Toho stagehand whose nickname was Gojira. The real name and company position of this original "Gojira" remains unknown which, as Guy Mariner has noted, "given the Japanese studio's penchant for keeping accurate records, further suggests the story is apocryphal. The name of whomever came up with Godzilla is lost in time as well, so ... at this point no explanation of either genesis is likely to be forthcoming" (6). In a 1998 BBC documentary Kimi Honda, director Ishiro Honda's widow, laughed off that story of the stagehand. "I believe it came out of serious meetings between my husband and the producers," she said.* In fact, no one in any position of authority ever explained how the name was decided. Honda's biographer Steve Ryfle admits that "the name's origins remain mysterious" (88).

I think, though, we do have some clues about the derivation of those two concluding syllables. Gojira's crooked jaw, seen clearly in his frontal closeup above Hachiman Hill on Odo Island during his first reveal, and on several occasions during his excursions through Tokyo, appears to be a sly reference to the *-jira* part of his name. Moby Dick, most monstrous of all fictional cetaceans, was also marked by his crooked jaw. Captain Ahab famously exhorts his sailors to sight the leviathan, making the

---

*See N.F. Jones' BBC documentary which also includes interviews with members of the original *Gojira* crew and cast.

Prologue: Monsters and Mythopoesis

following promise: "Whoever of ye raises me a white headed whale with a wrinkled brow and a crooked jaw" would win a gold coin he nailed to the mast. A partial translation of Melville's novel by Tomoji Abe appeared in Japan in 1940, another revised section in 1949, yet another in 1950, and a complete translation was finally published in 1954. Abe was highly visible in the country's literary and political circles before and after the war, not only one of Japan's most respected translators of western literature but a novelist and critic of stature. He was also the author of five original film stories from 1938 to 1955. As an anti-nuclear and anti-militarism essayist, his political and social opinions aligned him with Ishiro Honda's own brand of pacifistic humanism. His translation of the American masterpiece was anxiously anticipated by Japan's literary crowd.

We also know Honda was familiar with him. In 1950, the future director of *Gojira* worked on pre-production for a Toho project, *Shimbun koz (Newspaper Kid)*, based on an original story written by Abe (Ryfle 49–50) at the same time he was translating his third instalment of *Moby Dick*. Since *Gojira* story author Shigeru Kayama (the pen name of Kōji Yamada, born in 1904 in Tokyo) was also a fantasy and adventure novelist of stature, and given that Japan to this day retains its controversial whaling industry, it is likely at least two of the key contributors to *Gojira* were familiar with the translated American novel and incorporated that telltale deformity into the monster's physiognomy.

There are other noteworthy allusions to *Moby Dick* in *Gojira*. Like the tormented amputee Ahab who dies with his whale when it submerges, stabbing at it with his charmed harpoon, Dr. Daisuke Serizawa, who lost an eye in the late war, submerges and dies with his monster while activating his oxygen destroyer. As if to anticipate this analogy, the wrought iron guard framing the chemist's parlor window consists of rows of vertical rods ending in lanceolate, twin-fluted points, like a rack of harpoons. Tellingly, we see this window just after the journalist Hagiwara interviews Serizawa who, unsettled by the reporter's awareness of his research and his German connection, prepares to reveal the existence of his oxygen destroyer to his fiancée, Emiko (played by Momoko Kochi).

We see the window again later in the film when Emiko and her boyfriend Ogata confront the scientist about the existence of his weapon and urge him to use it against Gojira. I don't believe it is coincidental that the harpoon window guards recur on both occasions when the

Prologue: Monsters and Mythopoesis

oxygen destroyer is discussed. Bluntly put, the harpoons are meant to draw an analogy between hunting down Moby Dick and killing Gojira.

The film version of Melville's novel affords us another dollop of synchronicity. As Gregory Peck's Ahab plots on his sea charts his course to intercept the great whale, he informs Starbuck of his intention to encounter his quarry near Bikini—the site of the Crossroads and Castle series atomic and hydrogen bomb tests which rousted Gojira from his abyssal habitat in the first place. The island had been the site of American atomic bomb tests since 1946 so it was already enshrined in the popular nuclear ethos. Bikini does *not* appear in Melville's novel so one is left to wonder if its fissionable celebrity was behind screenwriters John Huston and Ray Bradbury's decision to make it the site of Ahab's fateful encounter with his whale. As if all this weren't enough, several critics have noted Gojira appears upon the centennial of Japan's opening to the west in an allegory of the destruction of traditional Japanese culture by westernization. Commodore Perry, it turns out, invited Herman Melville to accompany him before his *Kurofune*, or black ship fleet, kicked in the doors of *shokoku* Japan in 1853. Melville declined (Blouin 2).

During that fateful spring of 1956, American television ads for *Godzilla, King of the Monsters* featured a child's voice crying, "Wow! Look what's coming to our local theater! This movie I *gotta* see!" while Godzilla loomed over rooftops with his unforgettable honking roar. The ad grabbed me like a snapping turtle. That roar hooked a lot of other folks, too. Every kid in the neighborhood wanted to see it. The writers of a popular comic book contemporaneous with the film, Dell and later Gold Key Comics' *Turok, Son of Stone*, called their dinosaurs "honkers." I was by then a great aficionado of all things dinosaur and my room was a warehouse of picture books, plastic figurines, and poster versions of Knight murals.

My father took me to a Saturday matinee of *Godzilla, King of the Monsters* at the Strand Theater in Far Rockaway, New York, in May 1956, a few weeks shy of my sixth birthday. The Strand was an old theater with faded flock wallpaper, every bit as somber and brooding as those museum galleries even with its house lights on. It felt like the right place to see a dinosaur movie. We scored our popcorn, candy bars (I got a Clark Bar, now as rare yet defiant of extinction as a trilobite) and soda and took seats right in the middle of the orchestra. In the tradition of

Prologue: Monsters and Mythopoesis

those grindhouse years the Strand played double features on weekends, so I had to endure a western while waiting for the main event.

After sitting through a few trailers the house lights dimmed again as *Godzilla* finally unspooled. The hidden beast, that uncanny roar presaged a ragged font of the monster's name which appeared across a cauldron in the night sea. It was as spooky as the Cretaceous gallery but augmented with frightening sound effects. This dinosaur was not going to be a static display. Neither was it a smooth skinned, glistening brute like one of Knight's renderings. Its flesh was rucked and rumpled, its features deformed, its castellated back glowing as it spat its corrosive aerosol like a true Japanese dragon. It cooked and trampled buildings and people. Cannon fire only enraged it. I was transfixed.

Scenes of citizens fleeing before it framed from just behind its advancing feet were to haunt my dreams into adulthood. At six years old, I didn't follow the anti-nuclear, moral, or romantic subplots but even while appreciating its pure spectacle I could sense the film's pervasive melancholia. All that human damage—children watching their parents die in overcrowded hospitals as ambulances unloaded still more of the maimed and irradiated, some of whom cried out in pain—broke my heart. I didn't understand that its Japanese audience recognized those scenes from experience. Nevertheless, I felt like Prince Gautama must have when he wandered from the palace to encounter pain and death for the first time. Most of all, I remembered Ogata's portentous words, written by Hollywood lifer Al C. Ward for the partially dubbed soundtrack, as the young salvage diver struggled to convince a recalcitrant Serizawa to relinquish his oxygen destroyer: "You have your fear, which might become reality, and you have Godzilla, which *is* reality." That, I realized in some instinctive manner, was all the philosophy I would ever need.

The great Argentine fictionist Julio Cortázar recalled how "when I was a child and went to elementary school, my notion of the fantastic was very different from that of my classmates. For them the fantastic was something they had to reject because it had nothing to do with the truth, with life, with what they were studying and learning. When they said 'this movie is pure fantasy' what they meant was 'This movie is trash'" (35). My experience of *Godzilla* was much the same: it mattered to me in ways I understood it didn't to my peers. It still matters. I had occasion over the ensuing years to ponder the hold on my imagination this creature exercised, a hold which only strengthened while

Prologue: Monsters and Mythopoesis

other childhood and, eventually, adolescent preoccupations fell away. I don't know how many times I must have watched it on television. Unlike Jackie Paper, my magic dragon didn't yield to more mature preoccupations. Godzilla grew up with me. My interest in him, in the fascination he continued to elicit, sharpened while I studied mythology, psychology, politics and comparative religion.

Godzilla kindled my interest in all matters Japanese. Eventually he drew me to Japan. I traveled through the country several times dragging my family along with me, a scholarly tourist in search of a monster. When the hotel I booked for my first visit to Tokyo, the Shinagawa Prince, stood on the very hill from which Yamane, Shinkichi, and Ogata watched the creature emerge from Tokyo Bay and trample the rail yards, I felt engulfed by coincidence. By sheer luck a cab driver the hotel concierge recommended as a guide was a *kaiju* fan and sacrificed his street map to mark off Godzilla's route through the city. We followed it like some *tokusatsu* Way of Saint James.

Naturally, I made my pilgrimage to the Gojira statue in the plaza of Tokyo's central rail terminal, the very spot where, twenty years later, Shin Gojira would run out of steam and be unceremoniously frozen stiff. Onward, I visited the atomic parks and museums in Hiroshima and Nagasaki. Aside from a visit to Auschwitz or Dachau, you couldn't imagine a more sobering experience or a more sickening exposition of man's bottomless inhumanity. The dioramas of *hibakusha* wandering the ruins like ambulatory cinders contributed hugely to my comprehension of the impact *Gojira* must have had on its audience when it opened in Nagoya in October 1954.

Reading widely in Japanese literature, I was absorbed by the novels and stories of Ryūnosuke Akutagawa, Shusaku Endo, Seicho Matsumoto, Hyaaken Uchida, Kobo Abe, Haruki Murakami, Masuji Ibuse and, inevitably, Yukio Mishima. The latter's "Sea of Fertility" tetralogy arrested me with its accommodation of Japan's recent political history to the mythopoesis of its ancient rituals and lore, an amalgamation which became central to my understanding of why Godzilla has become such a polyvalent figure in that nation's—and the world's—popular culture. In fact Mishima loved *Gojira* when it opened, celebrating it in a critical review entitled "Gojira's Egg." He put his nationalistic ideological agenda behind it, as he always did, but his appreciation of the film was still more perspicacious than the response of most Japanese critics at the time.

Prologue: Monsters and Mythopoesis

I also studied foundational texts in Japanese drama like Zeami's *Fushikaden*, in religion and myth like the *Kojiki* and the *Nihon Shoki*, and spent hours watching its national cinema, absorbing its art, drama and dance. Belatedly, as a bucket list item, I began learning the Japanese language. I'm still plugging away at it.

Gojira has since exfoliated into a mind-boggling phenomenon. He presides over a marketplace of cartoons, comic books, figurines, friction toys, keychain maquettes, posters, novels, coloring books, how to draw books, tattoos, plushes, party costumes, t-shirts, blankets (my daughter, whom I created a Japanophile, bought me a comforter with Godzilla superimposed over Hokusai's *ukiyo-e* "Great Wave off Kanagawa"), and his ever-proliferating fan websites. As statues of various sizes, from one meter high pedestal mounts to life-sized busts looming above buildings or swallowing zipline riding tourists, Godzilla has become a tourist attraction or even a local creature-mascot, what the Japanese call *yuru-kayara*.

There have been over thirty sequels to the original film. I know those sequels have their enthusiastic partisans but I'm not one of them. I won't spend time denigrating those films since, at the very least, their sheer proliferation kept the franchise in view as critical attention to them also proliferated and eventually acknowledged the brilliance of the 1954 foundational work I want to consider in detail here. Hence, I focus below on Ishiro Honda's original, and on its uneasy dialogue with its 1956 Americanized version. I discuss Hideaki Anno's superb 2016 extended parody, *Shin Gojira*, and Takashi Yamazaki's stunning 2023 *Godzilla Minus One* in the concluding chapters. In a very real sense both are extended commentaries on Honda's seminal vision. Ignoring the "monsterverse" series of American Godzillas and Roland Emmerich's 1998 mutant iguana version, I do however consider later on what happens to our monster when he is disenfranchised from his Japanese context.

Wherever else my interests led me, in a persistent childhood unconscious data and perspectives went on constellating around the lumbering *kaiju* I first met on that distant summer afternoon. It was not until 1982 when *Gojira* was shown in New York as part of a festival of Japanese films that I finally got to see it unbowdlerized. I had read about its differences from the Americanized version but, even so, in its added depth and pathos it was a revelation.

Prologue: Monsters and Mythopoesis

All that notwithstanding, the incident which finally began to draw together my thoughts about Godzilla occurred right back at the American Museum of Natural History sometime during the fall of 2011. My wife and I took our young son and daughter there during a visit to the city. The catacombs which once enhanced the eeriness of primordial death were gone. They had been remodeled and were now light, airy, spacious—and, I thought, sterile. In this brave new post–Alvarez Hypothesis, post–Knight world the main dinosaur exhibits had been rearranged. No longer organized according to geological epochs, the rooms were now separately devoted to the two main dinosaur families, the saurischians and ornithischians, the latter accorded primacy since, after all, they were going to bequeath us birds. Even Brontosaurus had been taken from us by the power-crazed ephebes of molecular genetics and cladistics, subdivided into Camarasaurus and Apatosaurus (could they have picked more charmless names?).

Dinosaurs weren't even reptiles anymore. Their skeletons were posed in frozen kinesthesis, tails held high off the ground, crouched like Olympic sprinters at their starting blocks. Those venerable Knight murals were now curios, fossils themselves, indicative not of how their subjects *were* but of how wrong we had been. In those august chambers Huxley's victory was complete. The Wilberforces of paleontology had been vanquished.

One thing which hadn't changed, though, was that replica Tyrannosaurus skull encased in its floor-level plexiglass display. As we stood further down the gallery two young rabbis led a troupe of about a dozen Orthodox Jewish children with Down's Syndrome through the far portal. They clustered in their black coats around the skull while one of the rabbis patiently lectured, then waved them along. Something verging on preternatural told me to keep watching them. Eventually they moved away except for one child, youngest and smallest of the lot. He continued to stare transfixed, nose on with that brutish countenance, yet reverently, as though it were a *bimah*. Then he reached behind himself, underneath his coat and withdrew his *siddur*, his daily prayer book, from a back pocket. Holding it open before him in one hand, his other arm akimbo, he began *davening*, bowing and straightening, bowing and straightening.

The rabbi at the end of the group noticed he was a child short and spun around. When he saw the lad praying to the *rex* head his eyes

Prologue: Monsters and Mythopoesis

flashed with horror. Striding back to the boy, he gently put his arm around him and eased him away towards the group, returning the *siddur* to his pocket. He reminded me of my own father displacing me from my seat at the Strand Theater decades ago. Once back at the end of the line with his mentor ushering him from behind the boy turned to look at the skull receding in the distance. He continued looking back until they were out of sight around a corner.

I've thought about that episode countless times, recalling William Tsutsui's observation in the introduction to *In Godzilla's Footsteps* that "[Godzilla] remains ever available as a metaphor, ever compliant to interpretation and appropriation" (11). I don't dispute that. My boyhood impression of Godzilla, one which has persisted despite accretions of discrimination and critical training, was nevertheless not of a symbol or metaphor, not even of a "man in a rubber suit," but of something *real and alive*. I suspect my fellow critics who treat the monster seriously also believe that or at least *want* to, even though they hide their fancy behind an analytical façade. What did that child think he was looking at which inspired him to prayer? Something about the rex's size, its shape, its toothy rictus, engaged his sense of the holy, or the mythopoeic, such as he understood it to be. I suspect his experience of the monstrous was not so different from my own when I was his age. Vouchsafed an epiphany in puzzle form my thoughts would always bring me back to the King of the Monsters and his cultural milieu within which hell itself had been recent experience, dragons rampaged, and the demonic was an aspect of the divine. *Gojira* began to suggest itself as an anatomy of melancholia.

Joseph Campbell has called myths "energy releasing and directing signs."* In the sense that Gojira is based on a group of ancient Chinese and Japanese sea dragon myths, and has evolved a contemporary, transcultural mythos of his own as both Gojira and Godzilla, he also qualifies as such a sign. He has become a semiological problem and semiology, simply put, is the study of the language of signs. Jase Short framed the matter succinctly: "A creature with fantastic origins in local folklore of Pacific Islanders which has undergone a thorough science fictionalization at the hands of atomic testing became for the Japanese public a cultural cipher, or a symbol which could be readily

---

* See Campbell's introduction to *The Masks of God, Vol. I: Primitive Mythology* (New York: Viking, 1968) for his elaboration of this key premise.

Prologue: Monsters and Mythopoesis

understood as representative of something too vast and complex for a more realistic-oriented narrative" (66).

In what follows I propose to explore how a savvy director enables a monster to signify, concentrate, and focus anxieties at the heart of which cultural codes in crisis will inevitably be discerned. This book is no more nor less than my working out of the puzzle of Gojira. Some of it is necessarily speculative because much about Godzilla and the fascination he elicits is so complex that, in the end, one can only speculate. I have wherever possible tethered my speculation to history, science, and ultimately to myth. But it hasn't always been possible. Such is his enduring enigma.

A NOTE ABOUT GOJIRA/GODZILLA: When referring to Ishiro Honda's 1954 film, or Hideaki Anno's 2016 film, I have used the monster's original name, Gojira. When I am referring to the edited 1956 American version or Takashi Yamazaki's 2023 film, I have used Godzilla. I have preserved whichever name was used in any citations as I found them and used Godzilla in discussions about the creature as a cultural, religious or political metaphor independent of either film.

I

The Growth of Critical Response

> "Oh, they'll find him, all right. The big question is, will they kill him?"
> —Steve Martin

THERE AREN'T MANY ASPECTS OF *Gojira* which haven't been picked apart, parsed, analyzed, and re-interpreted by film critics, sociologists, psychologists, historians, or even literary critics who have wandered off their turf. The comment of American character Steve Martin (Raymond Burr) to his senior editor in Chicago, cited above, could be about this sprawling critical community as much as it is about the Japanese Coast Guard. The increasing recognition of *Gojira* as a true classic has not been an ideologically innocent process, though. Criticism did not suddenly appreciate, for example, Emiko's struggle with the masculine predetermination of her betrothal to Serizawa. Feminist critics, like mythographers, frame theorists, archetypologists, or formalists, had first to be convinced the film was a serious enough work to merit their serious attention. As that began to happen, each critical school lensed the filmic text through its own ideological bias. *Gojira* split into many wavelengths, like light through a prism.

As Steven Sanders has noted, "Many of the best science fiction films are thought to be allegories and have been interpreted symbolically.... However, it is controversial whether, or in what sense, such films treat social, political, or religious issues symbolically" (4). The privileging of *Gojira* and its descendants has been a product of arguments and discourses as various as the revaluation of science fiction itself. It has also been a byproduct of the enhanced cultural importance of myth and legend as revalued by Joseph Campbell and other mythologists, anthropologists, and psychologists, especially in terms of what qualifies as myth in the first place. As Jason Barr has written, "numerous kaiju films have eschewed science fiction trappings in favor of just these things: exhibitions of mythology, folklore, and fantasy" (8). In this connection some of the biggest shifts in how the film is regarded have to do with its mythic or legendary content and, thus, its role in shaping modern Japanese society. At the same time, as Jase Short has noted, "[Kaiju] are impacted by the world of radiation, environmental destruction, genetic engineering, and so on but carry with them a density which suggests they belong to the same world we inhabit" (67).

Peter H. Brothers, who has written a detailed account of the making of the film, contends that after all the years since its 1954 release "*Godzilla* is still a highly original work without precedent and not an easy film to define: part documentary, part social drama, part commentary, part allegory, part cautionary statement, and part monster movie" (*Mushroom Clouds and Mushroom Men* 72). Brothers mentions "monster movie" last, as though in order of importance. There's nothing ironic about this, although as a genre the monster movie is not necessarily limited to kitsch. For cinema historian and screenwriter Mallory O'Meara, "Monster stories are powerful. They explore prejudice, rejection, anger, and every imaginable negative aspect of living in society" (158). The disturbing experience viewers expect from the genre, which is what draws them to the cinema in the first place, is an unusually complex issue in this film. Its original audience was the Japan emerging from a bitter defeat and nuclear punishment less than a decade earlier. In Japanese terms, what was expected of *Gojira*? A potboiler like the western imports which had been so popular during the several preceding years, but which surprised by resurrecting recent experiences of horror?

Gojira, as I prefer to address the original version, including the creature on its own terms, has fans, scholars, and hybrids of both. It is a resonating chamber of symbolism plumbing the cultural ethos of the Japan of the time of its making, as well as an omnibus of moral conundrums with which technology has faced mankind in general. A putatively prehistoric creature deformed—if not many times enlarged—by nuclear radiation, Gojira is the fulcrum of the film's underlying theme of the cultural struggle between prewar and postwar Japan, or put another way, of an ancient civilization's misbegotten collision with modernity. "Literally born out of the ashes of WWII fire raids, indiscriminate

I. The Growth of Critical Response

radioactive fallout and nuclear disasters," Brothers opines, "*Gojira*—as with the monster itself—embraces multiple meanings, paradoxical undertones, and ciphers hidden in plain sight" (*Mushroom Clouds and Mushroom Men* xviii). And for Michael Dylan Foster, who has extensively studied the long Japanese tradition of spirit beings, demiurges, and monsters known collectively as *yōkai*, such creatures "are encoded with critical data from the cultures and times in which they thrived, and they can tell us about the values and beliefs of the people who created them" (*The Book of Yōkai* 59).

Cultural anthropologist David D. Gilmore has more broadly studied the roles of monsters and the monstrous in human civilization. He argues that

> for most people monsters are sources of identification and awe as well as of horror, and they serve also as vehicles for the expiation of guilt as well as aggression: there is a strong sense in which the monster is an incarnation of the urge for self-punishment and a unified metaphor for both sadism and victimization (after all, the horrible monster is always killed off, usually in the most gruesome manner imaginable, by humans). We have to address this issue of dualism, of emotive ambivalence, in which the monster stands for both the victim and the victimizer [4–5].

Gojira, in other words, is also a *portent*, like a nightmare broken loose from sleep. Consistent with nightmares which plague victims of post-traumatic stress disorder, the monster is, among many other expressions of trauma, a symptom of Japan's loss of the Pacific War and the terrible pounding it took in the process.

Or, we could view the beast as a communication from the unconscious from which consciousness cannot disconnect. As one critic put it, "[special effects director Eiji] Tsuburaya's images impress. They have a unique ability to stay with the moviegoer and burrow their way into one's subconscious. Moreover, these deathless images serve a story replete with tragic subtext courtesy of [director] Ishiro Honda" (Carrozza 84). The persistence of darkness and shadows in this film enhances the uncanniness of the creature as well. He lingers in our collective imagination like the aftermath of a bad dream and when we have bad dreams he often populates them. What could be more congruent with our nightmares than Godzilla?

Early in the last century psychoanalyst Ernest Jones wrote of the definitive terror out of his patients' dreams "whose eyes have the

In Search of Godzilla

phosphorescent glare of the sepulcher, and whose breath is poisonous as the marsh of Lerna. Everything horrible, disgusting or terrific in the physical or moral world, is brought before [the dreamer] in fearful array..." (17). Archetypal psychologist James Hillman describes "The classical nightmare" as "a dreadful visitation by a demon who forcibly oppresses the dreamer into paralysis, cuts off his breath" (37).

Godzilla conforms with some of the most often cited qualities of somnambulistic visitations, as though deliberately configured to lodge in our dreams. Scenes from his 1954 debut correspond with features of nightmare described by Freud, Jones, or Hillman: his pursuit of his victims is ponderous but irremediable; he threatens to crush if not consume them even if only by incineration with his radioactive breath. Turn around and he is right behind you. Break right or left to get out of his way and he collapses a building on you. The specter of his serrated mass rising at night from the waters of Tokyo Bay, off-balance yet relentless, is the quintessential traumatic nightmare percolating up from underneath the mind and troubling sleep.

There are many Freudian and Neo-Freudian etiologies of nightmare among the various schools of psychology. Not a few are mythographic, or descry connections between our darkest dreams and myths. Yet Gojira, devoid of any obvious connection with the libidinal energy Freud would insist upon, stands out in his asexuality, and with his kinship with toxicity or sterility rather than fertility. Even the commonplace gendering of Gojira as male, lacking as he does any visible genitalia, is a default to his behavior as alpha organism and is a social, not a biological, assessment. It devolves to the human figures within his ambit, in particular Emiko Yamane and her boyfriend Hideto Ogata, to endow the narrative with sexual memes. A salvage diver, Ogata is an avatar from the libidinal depths whose virility draws Emiko's desires free of their encumbrance by her childhood betrothal, though, as we discuss later, her desires are consistently deflected by the appearances of the monster.

Moreover, as I consider in greater detail below, Emiko's and Ogata's illicit relationship, a violation of Samurai class codes governing arranged marriages, parallels the advent of Gojira as a punishing figure and unfolds along with his story. If the beast is the post-traumatic nightmare of postwar and post–Occupation Japan, he is also this particular couple's nightmare in a special, if derivative, way. He thwarts their relationship repeatedly and forces them both to confront him—Emiko

I. The Growth of Critical Response

by running up Hachiman Hill on Odo Island unexpectedly to face him, then by revealing the existence of Serizawa's oxygen destroyer to Ogata—and Ogata by helping to carry the weapon directly into the monster's presence.

In his prologue to *Primitive Mythology* (1968), Joseph Campbell recounts that the nineteenth-century anthropologist Adolf Bastian distinguished between *elementargedanke*, or elementary ideas—a forerunner of C.G. Jung's "archetype"—and *volkergedanke*, or folk ideas, acculturated forms taken by the archetype in any particular tradition. Gojira started out as the monster from the Japanese Id. An expression of the totality of the nation's Pacific War related humiliation, wounds, and fears, he has graduated, so to speak, to the status of an archetype in his own right. As Gilmore puts it, "Surrounding the threatened ego, the composite monster unites the chaotic danger of the id and the punishing superego, the alpha and omega of the mental apparatus" (18).

The monster has also become so ingrained in western thinking about Japanese civilization as well as Japanese thinking about its own history that he's even become an anachronism. In the Japanese telefilm based on Nobel laureate Kazuo Ishiguro's novel *An Artist of the Floating World* for example, sometime during the late 1940s the protagonist, Masaji Ono, takes his grandson to a *kaiju* movie. This would be at least five years before *Gojira*, the nation's first such film, was even released. Thus, the movie resonates backward as well as forward in the *kairos*, or timeless mythic aspect, of Japanese culture.

Foster addresses the inextricability of spirit beings from the national cultures which engendered them:

> Most likely in every part of the globe, human beings have shaped mysterious and fearful phenomena into monsters and spirits as a way of making sense and meaning of their experiences. But the particular shapes such monsters and spirits assume are anything but universal. They are sculpted by the distinct cultures and societies in which they emerge, evolving through specific historical moments and with the changing desires and challenges of the people who tell their tales [*The Book of Yōkai* 33].

We are confronted here with a chicken-or-the-egg conundrum. Mustn't some universal sense of awe or dread be in play before any particular culture goes about sculpting its fears into specific forms? It is an open question which the film does not directly address. Professor Yamane approaches the issue when he suggests to the Diet committee considering the damage the as yet unidentified Gojira has inflicted on Odo Island a few nights earlier that there are many mysteries afoot in the world. Moreover, although there have been attempts to excavate Godzilla from his Japanese roots, especially the so-called "monsterverse" American films, there is something hopelessly kitschy about him when disenfranchised from his heritage. I believe, and argue, he remains quintessentially Japanese.

However, there is a flip side to this argument of which Foster reminds us: "Particularly as they become recognized in other countries as a distinct product of Japanese culture, *yōkai* [monstrous supernatural beings] are dangerously poised to be part of essentialist or orientalist discussions about 'weird,' 'wacky,' or 'inscrutable' Japan" (*The Book of Yōkai* 69). In a similar perspective staked out by Michael J. Blouin, Western conceptions of Japan are often overdetermined by cultural and political stereotypes: "Eager to establish a power dynamic with the archipelago, American audiences delight in transforming the complex country into a set of complex symbols signifying the primitive, the unknown, the completely irrational" (2). While keeping both of these cautionary observations in mind, I would nevertheless argue there is nothing "wacky" about the original Gojira; he was conceived, and realized, in a spirit of deadly seriousness. Nor, as I hope to show, is there anything finally "inscrutable" about him despite his complexity.

Another fascinating perspective on the monster is his incarnation not just of the Pacific War's nuclear climax, but of the war and Japan's defeat in more general terms. Yoshikuni Igarishi views Godzilla as an indelible memory, as well as an active reminder, of Japan's social and military disaster. "Markers of loss were quickly disappearing in the 1950s in Japan's cities and countryside; Godzilla returned to reinscribe loss on the urban surfaces" (121), he insists. As Japanese society strove to leave the war and its horrors behind, Godzilla emerged to keep them from forgetting. For Igarishi, it isn't only this particular monster who serves this function, but the entire genre of indigenous films he founded:

> In the 1950s ... monstrous bodies became replacements for tangible markers of loss. Memories of the war, even without specific markers, were still ubiquitous in postwar society. However, increasingly removed from the scene of destruction and devoid of particular references, the memories were transformed into amorphous destructive forces. Monstrous forms that defy human comprehension were burdened with the mission to represent memories of war loss [114].

I. The Growth of Critical Response

Igarishi seems to be taking his cue from Maurice Blanchot, who had written "The disaster is related to forgetfulness—forgetfulness without memory, the motionless retreat of what has not been treated—the immemorial, perhaps. To remember forgetfully: again, the outside" (Kindle ed. 178). Nevertheless Igarishi's is one of the most challenging views of why Gojira and his brethren exerted such an enduring hold over the Japanese imagination. In effect, he views the monster as post-traumatic stress disorder personified, broadening the sense in which director Ishiro Honda had said he wanted Gojira to make atomic radiation visible. Nearly seven decades since he appeared on the scene, this implicit radiophobia combined with battle fatigue is a perspective foreign viewers and fans of *kaiju eiga*, the tradition of the island nation's cinematic monsters, need to reach out with their imaginations across gulfs of culture and history in order to understand.

If I were to quibble with Igarishi's interpretation of the Godzilla phenomenon it would only be to point out an episode from slightly earlier than the 1950s. In June 1947, a handful of American servicemen—perhaps unsurprisingly from Los Angeles and Hollywood—perpetrated a hoax over WVTR, the allied occupation's official radio station. Inspired by Orson Welles' notorious 1938 *War of the Worlds* broadcast which panicked many in the United States, these tricksters aired a report that a sea monster had risen from Tokyo Bay and was attacking American troops. Their broadcast, laced with screams, gun and cannon fire, and other sound effects, would have impressed the Firesign Theatre in its heyday. Like the Welles fiasco it engendered hysteria throughout the city. A less than amused General MacArthur, who already had his hands full with war crimes trials and the promulgation of a new Japanese constitution, had the perpetrators reassigned to Korea, among other places (Gunerius; Harnisch).

Now, it's difficult to assess how much influence this episode might have had on *Gojira* producer Tomoyuki Tanaka's idea for a giant monster movie.* None of the principal creators of the film ever mentioned it.

---

* Takashi Yamazaki, auteur of 2023's *Godzilla Minus One*, set his reboot of the franchise in 1947, seven years before *Gojira* was released. He also made other period pieces about the immediate postwar period and its traumas, including *The Eternal Zero* and *The Great War of Archimedes*. As he was an avid chronicler of the events during the last year of the Pacific War and of the decade which followed, it is hard to imagine that, at the very least, he didn't know about this American prank. See my postscript at the back of the book for a more detailed discussion.

In Search of Godzilla

This was, first and foremost, an American prank. Regardless, we can discern behind that hoax the sensibility of Occupation Japan, with whatever ideas a national lore saturated with sea dragons and other mythical creatures might have exerted on a bunch of homesick Tinseltowners.

Combined with the Hollywood backgrounds of these radio jokesters, and an already existing cinematic tradition of monster inflicted urban mayhem stretching from 1925's *The Lost World* through 1933's *King Kong*, we detect all the same complexes of social, political, and cultural influences which would ripen into Ishiro Honda's and Eiji Tsuburaya's grand conception for *Gojra* seven years later. We also sniff the delicious irony of animator Willis O'Brien's stewardship of those early American monster movies, the same Willis O'Brien whose work on *King Kong* inspired a young Eiji Tsuburaya, *Gojira*'s special effects master, to dream of helming a giant monster film in the first place.

Perhaps most ironically, *Gojira* carries within itself, as it were, a reflexively critical dimension which lies behind it the way a differential equation subsumes a Mandelbrot set. The film's writers and directors had conflicting intentions for their characters and events. I have chosen, rather than spend too much time bogged down in matters of authorial intentionality, to let the text of the film itself disclose its hints and secrets. I have several texts to work from, but I've generally stuck with the finished 1954 (or 1956) film itself. I've mentioned its other versions where they shed some interesting lights on, and tensions which needed to be resolved within, the film itself.

Those versions include four pertinent written texts: Shigeru Kayama's original story treatment, *Purojekuto G-Sakuhin*,* which was the basis for director Ishiro Honda and screenwriter Takeo Murata's final screenplay. In Toho's marketing runup to the first public screening, "From July 17 to September 25, 1954, the broadcasting service Nippon Hōsō aired an eleven-installment radio version of the Godzilla story, and in early October 1954, even before Kayama saw his first private screening of the film, the publisher Iwaya Shoten published the radio drama as a stand-alone book titled *Kaijū Gojira* [*Godzilla, the kaiju*]" (Angles in Kayama 208). And then, in July 1955, Kayama published a revisionist novelization of the film, a retrospective differing in

---

* The text of Kayama's original treatment is included as Appendix B in Brothers, *Atomic Dreams*, 428–437 of the Kindle edition.

I. The Growth of Critical Response

some important ways from both his original treatment and the working screenplay.*

Kayama's subsequent novelization might even be viewed as an early act of critical revision. Taken together, these texts demonstrate that Gojira was evolving in the thoughts and designs of his creators even after filming and editing were completed. They also demonstrate, I think, that the monster was already working his mythopoetic influence even upon the imaginations of the men who thought him up in the first place. We will treat some of these evolutions, and proposed differences from what finally appeared on the screen, in the chapters below. However, it becomes clear that Gojira already posed problems of containment, as if his strength, malevolence, and unpredictable antipathies demanded reigning in from a narrative viewpoint as well as a military one. Ergo we shouldn't be surprised that he continues to influence his fans and critics seven decades later.

Beyond memories of the Pacific War and the nuclear threat, *Gojira* is also indebted to the ancient *Yamato* which bequeathed its art, mythology, and lore to the film's visual and narrative textures. Even those sources, however, won't fully account for how and why the monster means so many different things. "Godzilla has always been intertextual precisely because it has always broken free of attempts to enclose its semiotic wanderings in a single text," writes Aaron Gerow. "There have always been other contexts that problematize efforts to fix Godzilla's meaning ... offering an example of the historical struggles over what movies mean and who determines that" (63).

Rather than settle on any one of its manifold meanings, then, I would like to read this classic film on multiple levels, affording each its own validity. Stories about how *Gojira* was made are widely available. They only need re-telling here when necessary to support some argument about how we might "read" the film. For the most part I am interested in what *Gojira* tells us about itself. I believe much of what it tells is important.

---

* Shigeru Kayama, *Godzilla and Godzilla Raids Again*, tr. Jeffrey Angles (Minneapolis: U of Minnesota P, 2004).

II

A Tale of Two Directors

As the Allied occupation ended with the Treaty of San Francisco, Japanese filmmakers began to address the psychological, spiritual, and cultural ramifications of the atomic attacks on Hiroshima and Nagasaki, as well as the impact of the loss of the Pacific War. These had all been taboo subjects under the Allied occupation regime since the end of the war. A few intrepid filmmakers had attempted to document the horrors of the bombings only to find their work denied distribution or even confiscated by the Allied censors. With the lifting of censorship in April 1952, it was a new ballgame.

In August of that year the *Asahi Picture News* ran the first extended photo spread of the atomic devastation, including the ruins of the two cities and the wounds of the survivors (Rhoads et al. 66). Several Japanese documentaries and dramas concerning the atomic bombings were produced, notably Kaneto Shindō's *Children of Hiroshima*. The earliest films on the subject drew mixed reviews and poor distribution; *Children* wasn't shown in the U.S. until 2011. Then, in November 1954, Toho Studios released the first of two Japanese films with powerful anti-nuclear messages, Ishiro Honda's epic *Gojira*, known in the west by its Anglophone pronunciation *Godzilla*.

The Japanese speak of *tateme*, the mere appearance of things, and on the surface *Gojira* was a monster movie. In its *honne*, or substance, though, far from being a commercial science fiction potboiler like western monster movies of the same period, several of which inspired it, its scenes of radioactive devastation and human suffering revealed *Gojira* was a meditation on Japan's national trauma as well as the planetary threat posed by thermonuclear weapons. Ryfle put the pacifistic director's goals for the film most succinctly: "Honda took the basic trappings of a monster melodrama and produced a plea for sanity amid the madness of the nuclear arms race. *Godzilla* is his darkest work, a window on

II. A Tale of Two Directors

his fears" (85). It spoke of nuclear technology not only in direct fashion but also in the symbolic languages of Shinto and Buddhist myth. This was its enduring pathway into the cultural unconscious of its national audience.

Just as forcefully, it addressed the disintegration of traditional social norms, the victors' coerced de-linking of religious observation with chauvinism, and the breakdown of family hierarchies. *Gojira* was a scathing critique of how deeply the nuclear event had transfigured Japanese cultural conventions. In this, and in its unblinking depiction of the pain, the horror, and the suffering caused by its monster, *Gojira* was audacious, a far more serious and substantive artistic achievement than other monster films of its time. It wasn't until Shohei Imamura's 1989 film of Masuji Ibuse's novel *Black Rain* that another Japanese director would portray the spectacle of nuclear ruin so vividly. For all that, in 1954 it took nerve to envision a monster film, the very archetype of the cinematic potboiler, as serious commentary on anything. And yet "Science fiction films are not about science," wrote Susan Sontag. "They are about disaster, which is one of the oldest subjects of art" (213). Short echoes Sontag's view, and goes a few steps further:

> Art with a critical edge afflicts its audience. It challenges them to see the world in unique ways, and it does so in a way that is captivating. It does not lead one to "escape" reality, rather it warps that reality and presents it in a new configuration, more meaningful than immediate perceptions can afford. This is why millions of ordinary people in Japan found *Gojira* (1954) so moving, whereas a similar cross section of the population did not, for better or worse, engage in a campaign of active politicization in order to come to terms with the legacy of World War II. The catharsis experienced by those theatergoers can never be replicated, as it was a unique historical moment with a unique and new artistic object in play [69–70].

The other, less well known, antinuclear film of the period, which also sported a critical edge, was released a year after *Gojira*. Akira Kurosawa's *Record of a Living Being*, shown in the west seven years later as *I Live in Fear*, is the story of an aging industrialist whose obsession with the possibility of another nuclear war causes his psychological implosion. Just across the hall, so to speak, from where Honda's crew had created *Gojira*, Kurosawa was confronting the breakdown of Japanese family traditions even more forcefully. He was coming off the back-to-back triumphs of *Ikiru* and *The Seven Samurai* and had years of greatness ahead, so he was in many ways at the peak of his creative powers.

Record depicts the psychological collapse of a paterfamilias, instigated by radiophobia and by the machinations of his mercenary children and in-laws. They attempt to have the 70-year-old Nakajima declared incompetent to keep him from shutting down his factory, on the income from which they all depend, and emigrating to Brazil where he believes he will be safe from an inevitable thermonuclear war. Surely, the similarities between the family crises in both *Godzilla* and *Record of a Living Being* cannot be merely coincidental, and we might justifiably regard *Record* as Kurosawa's *Gojira*.

In the backwash of the occupation, the deliberate subversion of paternal authority by Allied decrees became a concern of both filmmakers. For Kurosawa, "anxieties about whether Japan could modernize and still remain essentially Japan helped to produce a cultural perception of modernity in ambivalent and, at times, negative terms" (Prince 312). When Nakajima prostrates himself before his horrified family, begging "please, please come to Brazil with me," it must have unsettled its audience, too. So must have the shadow which so often fell behind the old man, suggesting the fears which haunted him but also the way victims of the atomic bombings had been vaporized and reduced to shadows on masonry by the nuclear flash.

These same doubts and negative perceptions haunted Kurosawa's good friend Honda and are rife throughout *Gojira*. We could also detect an inside joke between Honda and Kurosawa that the name of the radiophobic 70-year-old protagonist of *Record of a Living Being*, in a stunning performance by 35-year-old Toshiro Mifune, is Nakajima. The actor who wore the Gojira suit for most of the filming was also named Nakajima. It isn't the most common name in the Tokyo phone book. Ironic, too, was the casting of Takashi Shimura, *Gojira*'s Professor Yamane, fresh from witnessing the monster's effect on Tokyo, as a member of the committee passing judgment on Nakajima's sanity. Shimura always brings his trademark *gravitas* to his roles, as though stamped into his sad features with their radiant probity. So much of *Gojira*'s freight of thoughtfulness depends on it.

The visions of both auteurs were conditioned by unsettling episodes from their youth. The close friends shared experiences of terror, one manmade, the other natural. Honda was a prisoner of war of the

II. A Tale of Two Directors

Soviet Army in China, which would have been punishing enough. As his widow Kimi told an interviewer from the British Broadcasting Corporation for Nick Freand Jones's 1998 Godzilla documentary, the experience remained with him for the rest of his life. Although it has been widely remarked that Honda passed through Hiroshima during his postwar repatriation journey, and what he saw motivated him to re-create his troubled vision in the devastated Tokyo of *Gojira*, much of Honda's view of the stricken city from his train was blocked by fences and barricades erected around the blast zone by the allied authorities (Ryfle 40). Whatever Honda beheld was undoubtedly bad enough, but then virtually every major Japanese city except Kyoto had been devastated by conventional bombings, including if not especially Tokyo in the March 1945 B-29 incendiary raids.

More likely the full horror of what happened in the atomic cities only became apparent to him later on, with the eventual release of photos, newsreel footage, the accounts of *hibakusha* and news of the still unfolding consequences of radiation sickness. Honda may have sublimated this sequence of revelations about just how bad it really was in the two scenes of Serizawa showing Emiko the effects of his oxygen destroyer. In the first, we know something awful has happened. We aren't vouchsafed a view of what it was until later, when she relates what she saw to Ogata at the hospital where she has been working as a volunteer.

In 1923 Kurosawa, at the age of 12, was walked through the ruins of Tokyo by his older brother Heigo just a few hours after the Great Kanto Earthquake, which killed nearly 143,000 Japanese. As recalled in his autobiography, he saw piles of human corpses set upon by birds and rats. Heigo refused to permit him to look away (Kurosawa 52).

Kurosawa had his own reasons to resent the Allied censors. His 1945 film *The Men who Tread on the Tiger's Tail*, set in the late 12th century, was banned for nearly seven years for supposedly extolling "feudal values" (Galbraith 63). An American animal rights activist—yes, we had them that long ago—harassed him legally over his scene of a panting dog which opened *Stray Dog* in 1949, baselessly accusing him of injecting the dog with rabies (Kurosawa 177).

What makes the tandem releases of these films even more interesting, aside from sharing key cast member Takashi Shimura, Honda and Kurosawa were close friends and collaborators. Honda was assistant director on *Stray Dog*, and later participated in comparably important ways in Kurosawa's last five films including *Kagemusha, Ran, Dreams*, one segment of which he directed, *Rhapsody in August*—which dealt with the Nagasaki atomic bombing—and *Madadayo*, a revisitation of life in the ruins of the postwar Tokyo Kurosawa had explored 23 years earlier in his underrated *Dodes'Ka-den*. Kurosawa, in turn, appeared on the sets of Honda's later projects as an uncredited assistant when his friend's declining health made it increasingly difficult to carry his directorial burdens alone. Kurosawa delivered the eulogy at Honda's funeral in 1993.

In his autobiography, Kurosawa related how much he depended on Honda's filmmaking skill, passion for detail, and integrity, to support his directorial efforts. You can sense the origins of the insights and vision implicit in Honda's depiction of the ruin of Tokyo in *Gojira* in his work as Kurosawa's *jokantoku* on *Stray Dog* five years before he filmed his masterpiece:

> Every day I told him what I wanted and he would go out into the ruins of post war Tokyo to film it. There are few men as honorable and reliable as Honda. He faithfully brought back exactly the footage I requested, so almost everything he shot was used in the final cut of the film. I'm often told that I captured the atmosphere of post-war Japan very well in *Stray Dog*, and if so I owe a great deal of that success to Honda [175–176].

Without gainsaying Honda's personal vision in the making of *Gojira*, it is difficult to believe he would not have discussed his film with his best friend and closest confidant. In fact I suspect Kurosawa had more input into Honda's thinking about *Gojira* than most critics have realized. Before Toho producer Tomoyuki Tanaka drafted him to direct *Gojira*, Honda worked closely with Kurosawa during what Brian Brems (2021) has described as Kurosawa's *noir* period. From 1948 to 1949 Kurosawa and Honda labored on the *noir*-influenced *Stray Dog*. He clearly benefited from observing his friend's creative processes and was determined to appropriate the same leeway for himself. Whispers of his great friend's work can be heard throughout Honda's project if one listens closely. An early scene in *Gojira* depicts Ogata and Emiko having to change their plans to attend a concert together, which recalls the aborted concert date of Yuzo and Masako in Kurosawa's 1947 *shomin geki*, or bourgeois slice of life, *One Wonderful Sunday*.

II. A Tale of Two Directors

In fact the way Gojira's repeated appearances disrupt Emiko and Ogata's efforts to reconcile their illicit relationship with Serizawa and with her father—a sequence of events considered in more detail below—echoes the string of complications thwarting the lovers of Kurosawa's romantic comedy. This is just one example of *Gojira*'s many intertextual features. "They may have treated auteur types [like Akira Kurosawa] differently," Honda said, "but for something like a science fiction movie putting thoughts or ideas into your movie was considered plain stupid" (Ryfle 47). Honda shrugged convention off. He was going to become an "auteur type" and shape the first *kaiju eiga* to his own vision.

Early on in *Gojira*'s production schedule Honda and special effects director Eiji Tsuburaya considered how best to bring their monster to life. They determined the studio couldn't afford, in terms of time or expense, stop motion animation in the style of Willis O'Brien's *King Kong* or Ray Harryhausen's *Beast from 20,000 Fathoms*. Quite a few critics have pointed out that *Gojira*'s frequent defaults to nighttime settings helped disguise the artificiality of its budget-conserving technique. Yes, it does. But the darkness contributed more than that. As Ryfle and Godziszewski observe, when *Gojira* was produced,

> Japanese films ... were still mostly made with 1930s vintage cameras and equipment, shot on monochrome and nitrate film stock in the Academy ratio. [Cinematographer Masao] Tamai used this aging technology to give *Godzilla* a moody, noirish look, unique among Honda's works. Many scenes take place at night or indoors, with low key lighting from a bonfire, searchlight, or streetlamp. Light streams in through windows, and high contrast shadows angle across walls and faces ... during Godzilla's nocturnal raids, the eerie black makes the monster's enormity all the more believable [90].

The film's repeated contrasts between light and darkness also background the moral conundrums faced by several of its characters, especially Serizawa, Yamane, and the surreptitious lovers Emiko and Ogata. Certainly, it emphasizes the ethical relativity of science which advanced man's knowledge of the way the world is made but also produced nuclear weapons out of that knowledge.

Stylistically, it gave Honda the opportunity to apply to his monster movie chiaroscuro lighting effects typical of *noir* detective films. With its monster depicted against a dark sky, the film's lighting and cinematography also evoke the shadowy washes of Japanese brush and ink painting. This would prove to be one of its qualitative distinctions, evoking an aesthetic convention already familiar to its audience. "Shadows are ubiquitous in *Godzilla* and as much attention was given them as illumination," notes Brothers (*Atomic Dreams* 107); "Filled with brilliantly crisp images, high-and-low contrasting light, and soft tonalities, *Godzilla* is the world's most beautifully photographed monster movie" (108).

During his attacks on Tokyo the monster literally progresses from obscurity in the distance and darkness to gradual revelation, which enhances the drama of his arrival. When Gojira rises from Tokyo Bay he is usually limned, more than illuminated, by moonlight or searchlights. At the beginning of his foray through the Shinagawa rail terminal he is a huge dark shape who eventually steps out of the shadows to reveal details of his physiognomy. We finally get to see him clearly when the commuter train slams into him and he picks up one of its cars in his jaws. As he releases it his eyes glare and we see his rows of crooked teeth, set against the deeper blackness of his mouth. When he turns to leave we get a good look at the rows of jagged plates down his back, now lit by searchlights and perhaps by a moon which has broken through an overcast sky much as he emerged from darkness himself.

Chiaroscuro is even more pronounced when *Gojira* trundles out of the bay a second time and approaches the high tension electric lines strung across his path to keep him out of the city. Searchlights fall on his torso from somewhere ahead of him, providing contrast between his gray bulk and his glowing abdomen—an artful, haunting contrast—as he pauses before the power cables and then quietly, almost thoughtfully, turns slowly back and forth. This pause ends with an ear-splitting roar as he contacts the lines, and multiple explosions as artillery bombards him. The searchlight beam is supplanted by sparking wires and flashes of cannon fire.

Soon afterwards we find ourselves sighting along a boulevard down which citizens flee as Gojira's arms and torso, lit around the edges of his body, slowly appear from our right filling the screen. And when he finally unleashes his radioactive breath, his dorsal plates light up, again in sharp contrast with his darkened body, emphasizing his size and mass. His extended nighttime assault features views of the monster as a shadowy figure set against fires engulfing the city in his wake. As J.L. Carrozza writes, "The special effects sequences in *Godzilla* stand among Eiji Tsuburaya's greatest cinematic triumphs. Shot on the silvery

II. A Tale of Two Directors

splendor of old-school nitrate film, his smoky, atmospheric monochrome images are phantasmagorical, unforgettable and iconic" (83).

While Honda incorporated noir elements into *Gojira*, which Tsuburaya to a lesser extent incorporated into its slapdash sequel *Godzilla Raids Again* (1955), the director then left the style behind as Tanaka tasked him with Godzilla sequels and other kaiju standards like *Rodan* (*Radon*, 1956) and *Mothra* (*Mosura*, 1961). Toho's kaiju films after *Raids Again* would all thenceforth be in color. Kurosawa, meanwhile, continued to work within the *noir* genre with *The Bad Sleep Well* (1960) and *High and Low* (1963).

Despite their difference in genre—one a *shomin-geki* or family drama, the other the first *kaiju eiga* or monster movie, *Record* and *Gojira* share many other essential concerns. That Godzilla incarnates nuclear anxiety and is a warning about the consequences of nuclear testing is by now a truism. Honda has said in the figure of the monster he "wanted to make radiation visible" (Galbraith et al., 21–22). Nevertheless, the family drama unfolding within *Gojira* bears much of its pathos and subtly communicates its extended warning, even as scenes of carnage and suffering communicate it overtly.

I suspect Kurosawa's influence can also be felt in the way the confused relations between the Yamane family, Ogata, and Serizawa play out so crucially for the resolution of the *kaiju* story engulfing them. Like the *noir* touches which add so much to *Gojira*, the disintegration of the family is a theme that Honda leaves behind as he segues into the string of *tokusatsu* follow-ups Toho assigned him afterwards. For Kurosawa, though, it was a recurrent issue, especially in *Ran*, his 1985 revisioning of *King Lear*, and in his late work, *Rhapsody in August* (1991), where nuclear memories return to play an important role. In *Gojira*, Honda was intent to demonstrate that nuclear anxiety strikes as deeply into culture as radiation penetrates to the genome. In *Record*, Kurosawa followed his lead.

These films also shared their depiction of radiation as myth. Radiophobia is a justifiable fear but at the same time many of the effects that science fiction films of the 1950s and 60s attributed to radiation were as opportunistic as they were apocryphal. The same was true of the attributions of popular culture, especially, and understandably, in postwar Japan. By the time Honda and Kurosawa made their films medical scientists were already aware of how virulently teratogenic radiation can be, but its cinematic ability to mutate organisms far exceeded what it could do in reality. The giant bug, the giant reptile, the resurrected prehistoric creature became standard motifs of the radiophobic genre of science fiction.

Although slightly earlier films like *The Beast from 20,000 Fathoms* showcased the power of nuclear testing to melt a lot of ice and bring prehistoric monsters back from suspended animation, *Gojira* and *Record* took harder, more interrogative looks at the recently decanted atomic genie. In other monster movies of the 1950s radiation was an all-purpose meme around which to build a B-movie screenplay. As Kalat noted, "In Japan, though, the case was different. Only the Japanese have directly experienced the horrors of nuclear war, and their perspective as victims of the atomic age carries deeper significance" (24).

Gojira, with its echoes of Buddhist and Shinto lore, plumbed that deeper significance by placing radiophobia at the service of mythopoesis. *Record* magnified radiophobia into its protagonist's obsessive, ultimately crippling, apocalyptic vision. For their time, both films stood alone in this regard. Americans suffered from the conceit they controlled the atom and so could enjoy its fanciful ramifications from a safe distance. This smugness, for that's what it was, doubtless accounts for the superficiality of so many western science fiction films. That the U.S. government kept a lid on information it was gathering about the long term effects of radiation poisoning contributed to keeping science fiction about anything to do with the subject naïve and even schlocky. As the Soviets exploded bigger and bigger test bombs of their own, however, that sense of American nuclear privilege dissipated. At the same time, it became politically useful to expose more of the horrors of nuclear weapons to mobilize public opinion in support of American cold war policies and, after a decade of alliance, to represent communism as a recrudescent threat. *Gojira*, meanwhile, had initiated in Japan, where the nightmarish aftereffects of nuclear weapons were already a felt reality, a cinematic trend towards peeling away political reluctance to engage the subject more honestly. In *Gojira*, the histrionics between left wing and conservative deputies in the Diet (beginning at 26:55) over how much publicly to blame hydrogen bomb testing for the monster's appearance is a case in point.

Whereas *Gojira* was a box office success, *Record* was not. It was in fact Kurosawa's first film to fail to recoup its production cost, despite

II. A Tale of Two Directors

earning excellent critical reviews. Stuart Galbraith, in his monumental study of Kurosawa and Toshiro Mifune, *The Emperor and the Wolf*, suggested *Gojira* had already exhausted the topic of nuclear anxiety for Japanese moviegoers (221–23). Perhaps, he speculates, the fantastical, or mythic, aspect of Honda's film buffered the unpleasantness of coping with such ugly memories and current realities alike. It was, after all, around the time these films were released the miserable long-term effects of the atomic bombings—cancer, birth defects not only among the survivors of the attacks but among their children as well—were becoming apparent. Professor Tanabe's grim expression as he examines a child survivor of Gojira's rampage with his Geiger counter (at 1:09:37) managed to express all of this in a short vignette. The comparative success of *Gojira* testifies to what a powerful and influential film it really was.

Occupation Blues

The nine-year lapse in responding cinematically to the atomic attacks on their cities is misleading on the face of it. While in the United States Hollywood wasted little time celebrating the Manhattan Project and the destruction of Hiroshima in films like Norman Frank's *Above and Beyond* (released in 1952), Japanese filmmakers weren't even allowed to mention the bombings, much less criticize them. Under the stiff censorship regime imposed by the victorious allies, they had little creative leeway to interpret their national nightmare. For over six years following the Japanese surrender American military censors patrolled Japanese cinema to assure nothing found its way out of a studio which might be conducive to insurrection, or which valorized the extinguished culture of imperial mysticism.

Ito Sueto tried to film a documentary, *The Effects of the Atomic Bomb on Hiroshima and Nagasaki*, as early as 1946. He must have thought the Occupation was kidding. It wasn't. The military censors confiscated every reel of the film except one which Sueto's Nichei Studio had hidden. None of it was seen until after 1952. Hideo Sekigawa filmed *Hiroshima* in 1953 using thousands of extras, many of them survivors of the bombing, but the film languished for want of distribution until re-released in 2014.

In Search of Godzilla

At the same time, the occupation authorities set out radically to restructure Japanese social and religious life. As Chon Noriega pointed out, the occupation

> dismantled and rebuilt the Japanese family and society.... Reform gave women full legal equality and ended the authority of the clan over the family and the father over adult children. Compulsory education was extended to nine years, further reducing parental influence.... For the most part, however, the Japanese cooperated with the Americans, bringing about enormous socioeconomic and political change during the relatively short occupation (1945–52). Such change, however much desired by both Japanese and Americans, required repression in order to succeed ... [65].

Even as the occupation transformed their culture, the Japanese artistic response to the disaster of the late war and to the imposed changes in their political, social, and spiritual life gave voice to the disorientation military defeat and social deconstruction had caused and were still causing. In *Censorship of Japanese Films During the US Occupation of Japan*, Lars-Martin Sorensen argues that Akira Kurosawa waged a guerrilla struggle, as it were, against the Allied prohibition of sympathizing with traditional Japanese cultural paradigms it disapproved of, as well as criticizing the censorship regime itself. One can tell when watching such films as Kurosawa's *Stray Dog* and *Ikiru* that criticism had to be subtle and implicit, like some Japanese celluloid version of *samizdat*, the Soviet-era protest literature.

The spring of resentment coiled tighter for seven years. As soon as censorship was lifted, Japan's film studios, underfunded, technologically backward compared to Western studios, got about the hard work of examining what was left of the country's prewar traditions. *Gojira* and *Record* emerged almost as quickly as production schedules permitted once military oversight ended. After April 1952, when the Treaty of San Francisco lifted censorship and restored Japanese sovereignty, Toho took a gamble on *Gojira* which, like Kurosawa's *Seven Samurai* over whose production schedule it overlapped, was one of the most expensive productions in its history. Despite its gravity and its subtexts of traumatic memories, or perhaps even because of them, it proved a box office bonanza.

Although Kurosawa and Honda both experienced the anguish of Japan's defeat, they nevertheless came to believe, like many Japanese, that the individual conscience must take precedence over the *Bushido*

II. A Tale of Two Directors

code. They understood traditions for which they still held affection would be lost in the cultural transformations then underway. At the conclusion of *The Seven Samurai* Kombei Shimada realizes the real winners of their war with the bandits were the farmers with their orderly lives. He thereby acknowledges the end of the era of mystified martial glory. Shimada, reduced once again to an unemployed *ronin*, appreciates the demise of his warrior class is the price of peace and security, to live creatively as opposed to destructively. This message resonated as intensely for the Japanese audiences of 1954 as would *Gojira*'s allusions to the late war.

One of his earlier films, *Stray Dog* (1949), had demonstrated Kurosawa's concern with the effects of defeat and imposed westernization. In an example of how closely they worked together, Honda designed and shot the sequence wherein Toshiro Mifune, as a young detective, searches the makeshift stalls and jerrybuilt black markets and back alleys of bombed-out Tokyo for his stolen pistol. A startling episode with street sounds but no dialog, it took the pulse of a defeated Japan while ogling the wreckage of its social and cultural life. The directors' mutual sensitivity to the ebb of tradition is further discernible in the narratives of *Gojira* and *Record of a Living Being*. Both films are valedictories to traditional culture and both represent the nuclear weapon as an encompassing menace.

What distinguishes them is the way *Record* holds nuclear anxiety in the background while it foregrounds the corrosive impact of western style materialism on paterfamilial respect. Nakajima's family mocks the old man's radiophobia, while *Gojira* holds the nuclear menace before us in the form of its *kaiju*, and utilizes mythological, folk, and religious imagery to bare a blistered national soul. Much has been written about the historical and geopolitical themes so immediately apparent in *Gojira:* radiophobia, the dangers of nuclear testing, and the still vivid memories of the destruction of Japanese cities by both atomic and conventional means. However, as Tsutsui writes,

> Japanese traditional art and literature, so scholars tell us, boasted bizarre supernatural demons and monsters.... Giant serpent deities inhabited remote mountain valleys, and dragons moved across water, land and sky.... In Godzilla one senses the echoes of such legendary beasts, awe inspiring and ever threatening, associated with the oceans, with longevity, and above all with ruin and calamity [15–16].

In Search of Godzilla

So whereas prehistoric monster movies were primarily a science fiction genre in the west, in Japan *Gojira* demonstrated such creatures were at least as much a mythic or religious genre. Unlike other cinematic dinosaurs of the same period, "Godzilla is a malevolent deity or genie" (Tanaka 61). Tanaka calls attention to the suggestiveness of the syllable "God" in the anglicized pronunciation of *Gojira*. The supposedly anglicized name of the monster was in fact a suggestion by the Toho marketing division to their American distributors. Joyce E. Boss observes how Godzilla resembles traditional Shinto nature deities, or *kami*. The monster "is associated with *kami*-like qualities.... [his] approach is signaled by shaking earth ... and often by a howling storm of wind and water—in other words, earthquakes and typhoons, which enjoy a deeply traditional association with *kami*" (105). And for Michael J. Blouin, Godzilla is "a giant amalgamation of the nuclear event and primal myths of Japanese lore" (88).

Ironically, then, Godzilla, among many other attributes, resurrects ancient beliefs whose hold on the popular imagination the Occupation reforms were intended to loosen, if not break. Honda, who grew up in a temple compound as the son of a Buddhist abbot, and his composer Akira Ifukube, the son of a Shinto shrine keeper, would have both been especially sensitive to possibilities for religious commentary inherent in their project.

Despite the cooperation cited by Noriega, it would be naïve to assume there was little resentment or resistance to the allied restructuring of Japanese society. In literature the urge to resurrect the militaristic nationalism of Japanese traditions repressed first by censorship, subsequently by consumerism, had its partisan in novelist Yukio Mishima. Mishima not only glorified *bushido* in his fiction and essays, most notably in his novel *Runaway Horses*, but tragicomically acted it out in his public *seppuku* (see Rankin, Chapter 7). However, the subliminal deconstruction of pre- and postwar culture by *Gojira* has rarely been discussed beyond the monster's incarnation of the nuclear event. Even less remarked is how consistently the movie alludes, whether deliberately or in those inescapable ways the cultural unconscious influences the creative imagination, to elements of Japanese family mores, religious traditions, and folklore. Let's discuss them now.

III

Dramatis Personae

EVEN THOUGH SEVERAL CRITICS HAVE at least broached the subject of *Gojira*'s indebtedness to Japanese myth, folklore, and religious practice, less has been written about the film's more subtle critique of traditions unraveling under the impact of enforced or consumer-driven westernization. *Gojira* is enriched by Honda's depiction of the family of its conflicted protagonist, Professor Yamane, an aging scientist caught between his empiricism and deeply felt emotions inspired by tradition. As a matter of fact one of the film's most unique aspects is the way its characters mature and change when confronted with the anomaly of Gojira's intervention. This concern with their personal evolution sets *Gojira* apart from a genre populated with static personalities. I have called *Gojira* a sad film and the remarkable face of Takashi Shimura as Yamane vectors so much of its sadness. The film's melancholy undertone is persistently elegiac, a paean to an older Japan in a state of decomposition.

The aged paleontologist's scientific interests link him to a geological past in a continuing process of recession. Meanwhile his culture's passing rituals—from the Odo Island exorcism ceremony which is a mere residue of ancient sacrificial rites, to the Samurai class arranged engagement between Emiko and Serizawa which has fallen apart—are borne by Yamane's downcast expressions and often slumping shoulders. The figure of the eminent scientists appears to be based on the Japanese paleontologist and author Matajirō Yokoyama (1860–1942), whose *Zensekaishi* (*A Prehistory of the World*) was, according to Jeffrey Angles, a formative influence on novelist Shigeru Kayama as a student. Kayama was to become the author of the original Gojira story treatment (Kayama 190).

Emiko Yamane, daughter of this eminent zoologist and paleontologist, rejects her betrothal as a child to Daisuke Serizawa and embarks on an illicit relationship. Her abandonment of her fiancé for the marine officer Ogata, which could easily have been made ancillary, is instead the film's pivotal narrative. More than that, Emiko prefigures the postwar Japanese woman in transition from subservience to feudal-era restrictions to self-determination. Mallory O'Meara has discussed in detail the sublimation of socially ambient misogyny into the roles of women in monster and horror movies as victims, screamers and leg-kickers. Jason Barr agrees, noting that "the role of women and gender in the kaiju genre remains woefully underexamined" (156). Barr continues,

> What, then, to make of the role of the female in kaiju film? In many cases, there are precious few examples, and those few examples are often depictions of women as bad, ineffectual, hollow, smitten, or some caustic mixture thereof. As we will see, even when many kaiju films attempt to place female characters in the foreground ... these women still somehow end up disappearing or fading into often disquieting stereotypes [157].

Emiko is visibly migrating off the cusp of precisely that stereotype. However, Barr doesn't mention Emiko, whose type of quietly yet insistently defiant character remains an outlier in later Kaiju films—another example of what makes *Gojira* so extraordinary. What's more, Emiko is a fulcrum of larger issue concerning changes in Japanese social codes following the Pacific War.

Originally, Honda intended to include, and actually filmed, idyllic scenes of the young Emiko and Serizawa together before the war (Brothers, *Atomic Dreams* 40) to add pathos to the disintegration of their relationship but decided not to include these vignettes in the finished production. No doubt he realized Serizawa, having not yet lost his eye, would have been much younger—too much younger to have risen to prominence within nine years, or so quickly accrued the funding for his independent laboratory under economically challenging postwar conditions—and scrapped the idea.

But there's more to Honda and screenwriter Murata's decision to frame Emiko and Ogata's illicit relationship the way they did. As it did in America, the war and its demands on the labor market expanded the opportunities for, and responsibilities of, women. Honda watched his friend Kurosawa exploit this theme in his 1946 masterpiece *No Regrets for Our Youth*, his first postwar, early occupation film. Emiko is prefigured by its heroine Yukie, also the daughter of a college professor.

III. Dramatis Personae

Her difficult progress toward strength and self-sufficiency vivifies the narrative.

Moreover, in the years before *Gojira* was conceived by its creators, a tearjerker radio soap opera based on a British wartime soap opera, *Waterloo Bridge*, had become an enormous hit. Premiering in 1952, *Kimi No Na Wa* (*What is your name?*), was one of the first popular postwar radio soap operas and arguably the most successful. The star-crossed lovers who met in a bomb shelter during the Operation Meetinghouse firebombings chose to meet periodically on the Sukiyabashi bridge, over which Gojira would stroll and destroy on his march into the Ginza district. Unfortunately the woman, Machiko, has been forced into a loveless marriage and the two can only meet on the bridge to express their unconsummated love.* They could be considered templates for Emiko and Ogata, whose romance, as we shall discuss below, was repeatedly interdicted by Gojira. The decision Honda and Murata made to make them lovers was, I believe, an effort to surf the popularity of *Kimi No Na Wa* at a time when it was at the peak of its popularity. Less than a year later, when original *Gojira* story author Shigeru Kayama's novelization of the film was published, the lovers had been readjusted to mere friends.

When the post-occupation government calls upon Emiko's father to join its blue-ribbon committee studying ship disasters near the coast of Japan, his involvement in the Gojira crisis unfolds simultaneously with Emiko's decision to defy his wishes, ignore her imposed engagement, and marry Ogata instead. Her behavior not only exemplifies the determination of allied occupation cultural policy to weaken a broad field of traditional Japanese family and social practices, but it also channels Ishiro Honda's own ideas about personal freedom.

As Ryfle tells us, "On matters of love and marriage Honda was a nontraditionalist, uncomfortable with arranged marriage and the way young people's feelings are ignored as parents and go-betweens force strangers into unions for reasons of economics, class status, and the continuity of bloodlines" (123). Honda and his wife Kimi married without parental approval and had to struggle. At the same time, Honda was no one dimensional moralist. Whereas Emiko is admirable in her

---

* See https://ourculturemag.com/2021/07/29/what-is-your-name-commercialism-and-modernity-in-postwar-japan/ for details about the radio program and the pop cultural phenomenon it became.

In Search of Godzilla

determination to lead her life according to her passions, her breakout entails ethical conundrums she cannot always navigate successfully. As a master metaphor for many of the social, political and psychological themes swirling through the vortex of *Gojira*, the monster also inflects several of Emiko's steps and missteps.

For one thing, the unraveling of her arranged betrothal parallels the appearance and fate of the monster itself. Emiko's awakening to *ren'ai*, or romantic love, in defiance of the 400-year-old Samurai class tradition of *omiai*, or arranged betrothal, coincides with Gojira's emergence from his abyssal habitat. In the film's opening scene, the panicking sailors aboard the *Eiko Maru* knock over a Go board, scattering its stones across the deck. Immediately, another crewman drops his guitar across the fallen board. The camera lingers for a moment on this telling vignette, the western instrument superimposed upon the traditional board game. However, given the significance of Emiko Yamane's violation of her arranged betrothal to Serizwa, it is fascinating to note that *miai* also denotes the matched arrangements of stones on the Go board. This opening *tableau vivant* subtly announces several key themes which weave through *Gojira* from beginning to end.

In a perhaps inadvertently comical sense, the monster with his mythic correspondences to ancient Japanese dragon lore is a warped symbol of tradition who keeps getting in the way of her anti-traditional romance with Ogata. When we first meet the couple, the sinking of the *Eiko Maru* has interrupted their concert date as Ogata must go instead to his employer's office. Following their trip to Odo Island, as Emiko and Ogata discuss resolving their triangle with Serizawa, the journalist Hagiwara bursts into Ogata's office to ask Emiko to introduce him to her fiancé. The reporter has been assigned to interview him about a rumored project which could be used against Gojira.

Later, when Emiko returns from having failed to inform her fiancé she is ending their betrothal, Gojira emerges from Tokyo Bay whereupon Ogata runs off to have a look before they can discuss what did or didn't happen. Perhaps no more than a day later, fecklessly attempting to request Dr. Yamane's consent to dissolve Emiko's betrothal amid his funk about the JDF's intention to kill off Gojira, Ogata insults her father instead by disputing the elder's desire to preserve the monster for science. Yamane orders the upstart from his home, stalking angrily off to his study. Sure enough, just as they seem ready to discuss where this

III. Dramatis Personae

latest peccadillo leaves them, the radio announces Gojira has chosen that moment to emerge from the Bay again.

Professor Yamane's anger is matched by his sadness over political and military forces conspiring to rob him of a scientific opportunity he never could have anticipated and believes will never come again. The elderly scientist has spent his life studying creatures who have ceased to exist, and suddenly he is presented by fate with a living, breathing (if not deformed) specimen out of his dreams. There is more than a hint of his fascination with ancient life in the way he ignores the danger of radiation poisoning by holding in his hand the trilobite he discovers in Gojira's footprint on Odo Island and then, having been warned by Professor Tanabe about it, eagerly prowls through the contaminated footprint for more of them. It is a poignant tableau.

When Yamane argues with Ogata about the merits of preserving the creature, he makes clear his nationalism wasn't killed off by the war. "No scientist in the world has ever seen anything like Gojira," he protests, describing it as "a priceless specimen found only in Japan." The trilobite may have been a fabulous discovery at the time but has become merely a consolation prize when he realizes the bigger prize will be denied him. Mike Bogue has suggested that "perhaps Dr. Yamane's plea to study Godzilla symbolizes a call to study Japan to see how it survived irradiation in 1945 and thereafter. But just as Godzilla is an atomic distortion of the former animal, perhaps post-war Japan is a distortion of its former self, having embraced the western mindset to the possible detriment of its cultural past" (171). Does this imply Yamane feels the rush to slay Gojira is an expression of "western" thinking? He already knows about the terrible human toll the creature has exacted upon Japanese merchant marine and fishing vessels. As a witness to the destruction on Odo Island, he is aware of the death toll the monster inflicted there. He has watched it kill dozens of commuter train passengers, and he has seen the even greater damage it could inflict prefigured in the Shinagawa rail yards. Still, in his argument with Ogata he remains unmoved. Aside from the incipient chauvinism of his comments, his idea of science is chillingly amoral—the antithesis, on the surface at least, of Serizawa's guilt ridden humanism, which will be explored shortly. Even so, he is not as extreme in his concerns as the writers of the film initially configured him. In Shigeru Kayama's story treatment Yamane had been represented as even more obsessed than in

In Search of Godzilla

Takeo Murata's working script, going so far as sneaking into the Tokyo power station controlling the high tension barrier against the monster and attempting to smash the control panel.

Yamane reappears onscreen just as Gojira concludes his second rampage through Tokyo. The professor has made his way to the harborside with Emiko, Ogata, and Shinkichi. Apparently, his anger at Ogata has been subsumed by the terrible events of this night. From the docks he watches Gojira wading down the Sumidagawa, at whose mouth the beast topples a span of the Kachidoki Bridge and escapes into the deeper water of the Bay. Tokyo burns in the background, a conflagration reminiscent of the March 10, 1945, American incendiary bombing of the city which ranked just behind the atomic attacks as a national trauma. His expression, like those of Ogata and Emiko, is a mix of horror and resignation. We can be pretty sure after the night's catastrophe he no longer believes Gojira can be studied like some outsized laboratory specimen.

Doubtless the revelation of the monster's radioactive breath has been a large part of what changes his mind. Gojira no longer merely emits radiation, he projects it. Although it may seem odd that even after Gojira revealed himself to be the cause of those many shipping disasters in the waters around Odo Island no one had thought to question by what agency the disasters were promulgated. The creature's deployment of his dragonlike capabilities was likely the paleontologist's emotional tipping point. It emphasized Ogata's concerns, expressed in his abortive argument with Yamane, that Gojira was "no different than the hydrogen bomb which still haunts us Japanese." Of all the key figures assembled on that dockside only the face of Shinkichi, who had seen his brother and mother trampled by the monster back on Odo Island, is contorted with impotent fury.

As Gojira disappears into the bay all Yamane can do is exhale. Honda chose Shimura-San for his ability to convey complex emotions with only subtle alterations of expression. We won't see him again until the last scene of the film. Meanwhile we hear a news bulletin while his daughter is working as a hospital volunteer, which announces he is heading up a commission to find countermeasures against another onslaught.

In the film's final scene, he is aboard the coast guard vessel bringing Ogata and Serizawa to deploy the oxygen destroyer, having finally realized the beast must be killed. Actively participating in Ogata's and

III. Dramatis Personae

Serizawa's assault on the monster, he also suffers the sickening realization his would-be son-in-law has severed his air and safety line like some latter-day Ahab, electing to die with the creature. Yamane's closing words are not merely a caution against further nuclear testing. In an exposition of how completely his view of Gojira has changed, he warns there are probably more of his species and that another one might be driven to the surface.

While the professor mutters this warning to himself the physicist Tanabe, who has been his atomic shadow, as it were, gets up from where he had been sitting morosely behind Yamane and walks away. With Gojira dead, Tanabe's services have become irrelevant. As the crew and passengers of the vessel stand at attention and salute their fallen hero, Yamane, his shoulders slumped, walks despondently across the deck in the background.

Yamane slowly evolves into a deeply tragic figure and I think his tragedy is meant to incarnate the tragedy of lost *Yamato*. An eminent scientist whose expertise has been devalued to a hunter or assassin, an expert who can't convince a soldier to inform his commander to stop shining lights in Gojira's eyes (as a group of news photographers are going to discover the hard way later on), a respected paterfamilias whose daughter has violated the terms of betrothal he had established years earlier, we see his reputation and authority decline over the course of the film. By the end of *Gojira* his moral transformation is complete. From bitterness over the prospect of losing his prize specimen, having seen the only countermeasure against the creature lost to any future emergencies, he is now oppressed by the fear another such monster will appear.

Emiko and Ogata aren't static personalities either. In contrast to Yamane they evolve throughout the film, and their growth is important to its resolution. Honda uses them, quite explicitly, to interrogate other aspects of a Japanese society struggling into modernity. When we meet them they are already carrying on their affair and have only just begun to discuss what they're going to do about her engagement. Emiko, from the outset, seems at peace with herself over their relationship behind Serizawa's back and even right in front of him, as when she stands beside Ogata on the deck of the research vessel to Odo Island, smiling and waving at him while crying "See you soon!" She's a cool customer, that one.

In Search of Godzilla

Emiko is complicated, a conflicted model of the emerging modern Japanese woman. We might guess she is well educated, first because she is the daughter of an academic but her sophisticated tastes are also indicated by her interrupted date to see the Budapest String Quartet with Ogata. She plays the traditional daughter, too. Serving her father beverages upon his return from meeting the security officials, she kneels before him and removes his jacket, and acts as his amanuensis during and after the Odo Island expedition. Emiko also demonstrates an all too familiar monster movie heroine proclivity for tripping, falling and screaming at just the wrong time during her panicked retreat from Gojira when it rises above Hachiman Hill, whereupon Ogata gathers her up and they duck behind some bushes. We do get some sense of her resilience when, a few moments later, she runs right back up the hill with her father for another look at the creature.

At the same time she is determined not to dwindle into Serizawa's lab widow, which begs the question of just how much affection obtains between her and her official betrothed. Since she likely had no input into her engagement, she feels little obligation to observe its traditional decorum and makes clear to her chosen lover she has always regarded Serizawa as an older brother. She also assumes the role of controlling partner in her new relationship. As she leaves her boyfriend's office with the journalist Hagiwara for what will prove to be an abortive interview with her fiancé, she rejects Ogata's offer to go with her so they can break the bad news to Serizawa together, saying "it will be easier on him if he hears it from me."

Emiko grows in purposefulness as a result of her hospital work in the wake of the destruction of Tokyo. We watch as the carnage brutalizes her conscience. Her father's colleague, radiologist Professor Tanabe, examines a child with his Geiger counter and then meets Emiko's gaze, shaking his head slightly to let her know the boy has received a critical dose of radiation. Shortly thereafter, gathering up a little girl who has just watched her unconscious mother being carried away on a stretcher, her face is a mask of anguish. At that moment Ogata climbs the stairs to her makeshift ward, also visibly shaken by the spectacle unfolding around him.

Moments like these incubate the real pathos and dramatic power of *Gojira* and elevate its *gravitas* beyond most other genre films. In contrast to her dismissal of Ogata's offer to accompany her to Serizawa

III. Dramatis Personae

a few days earlier, now she seeks his help to convince the scientist to make the oxygen destroyer available. I don't think there's any question she understands that by doing so she will, finally, expose her infidelity as well as break her promise to keep her fiancé's horrifying weapon a secret. Face to face with Serizawa, this time supported by her lover's presence, she finds the conviction to unburden herself. When she breaks down in tears as Serizawa burns his notes, she is not only crying over her apostasy, but appreciating the emotional harm she has done to a man she admires, respects and has loved like a brother, a man who has never done anything to deserve the pain she has caused him. It is her moment of coming *via negativa* into the fullness of her personhood.

Ultimately, though, the compounding of Emiko's bad faith in her betrayal with Ogata and then her revelation of the oxygen destroyer to him catches up with her. In her final scene we see her paying for her bad faith as she falls to the deck of the ship and cries. She is an intelligent woman who must be alert to the role her betrayal has played in her erstwhile fiancé's suicide. No one comforts her. She, like the Japan for whom Gojira was in his nuclear-mutated violence the final blow of the war that nation initiated, is entitled to the fullness of her guilt.

Ogata, too, outgrows his solipsistic, if not boobish, nature. With his country panicking and Gojira an impending menace he seems oblivious to the crisis, preoccupied instead with sorting out his love life with Emiko. To be fair, he had already voiced ethical concerns about their relationship which she had not expressed herself. On the research vessel en route to Odo Island, he tells Emiko he was surprised to see Serizawa on the pier to wish her bon voyage. The scientist's presence has made him uneasy. "Perhaps it was a final farewell," he tells her, meaning as much seeing them together has given away their liaison as that they are sailing a dangerous route.

Later, sitting in his office as he and Emiko discuss coming clean to her betrothed, he says "We've done nothing to be ashamed of," which sounds like he's trying to convince himself more than her, "but whenever I think of Serizawa I lose my nerve. If not for the war he wouldn't have lost his eye." Emiko, who as we have noted thus far hasn't expressed any misgivings about their conduct herself, then needs to reassure him her feelings about Serizawa have always been platonic. This visibly relieves her boyfriend who, if you'll pardon the expression, was fishing for it.

In Search of Godzilla

There is more to this vignette, however. Emiko's assertion that Serizawa's lost eye and facial scarring has nothing to do with her rejection of their betrothal is a threefold engagement with the current state of Japanese culture. Emphasizing her attempt to break free of parental choice made without her consent, it also represents a turning away from the spiritual scars of the Pacific War (of which Gojira represents the difficulty, writ large), and also the problem of the *hibakusha*, the often ostracized survivors of the twin atomic bombings. That Ogata brings it up is also subtly critical of Japanese society's fear and rejection of the atomic bomb survivors with their scars, radiation sickness and deformed offspring. Although we aren't told explicitly how the chemist was disfigured, as discussed below his character is also resonates on several levels of his nation's wartime experience.

In another tell we see Ogata looking out Dr. Yamane's living room picture window towards Tokyo Bay where searchlight beams are casting anxiously to locate the monster as soon as it breeches again. With the city on the cusp of destruction he smiles ruefully, turns to Emiko and announces he intends to ask her father for permission to marry her. He's gotten nowhere waiting for Emiko to break her engagement and has apparently decided to take matters into his own hands. It's as if the ongoing apocalypse were some mere distraction on network news. His intentions backfire when he is instead drawn cluelessly into an argument over Yamane's desire to protect Gojira from the military.

The monster's destruction of the city, and the misery Ogata encounters afterwards at the hospital full of refugees, refocuses the sailor. He forthrightly takes Emiko's part in their subsequent confrontation with Serizawa. It is Ogata, not Emiko, who asks him to use the weapon, who argues most convincingly about using it, and who apologizes on her behalf for breaking her promise of secrecy. He, too, comes fully into his own when he insists upon joining Serizawa in descending into the bay and placing the oxygen destroyer literally at the monster's feet, an act which, given how much he has seen of its destructive power and what he knows about its radioactive hazard, requires enormous courage. He is a young man who grows up before our eyes during Gojira's rampage.

I am hardly the first critic to observe that Daisuke Serizawa is the most complex and conflicted character in this film. Sigmund Shen asserts, "Tormented as Serizawa has been by the burden of his secret

III. Dramatis Personae

research, it is his fiancée's betrayal of that secret to her true love, Ogata, that makes him realize, for the first time in his life, how alone he truly is" (97). Whereas her betrayal may well have left the chemist feeling isolated and even humiliated, I don't necessarily believe his sense of isolation was all that new. The way he sequesters himself in the basement of his fortress-like institute, and the claustrophobic staircase he must descend to access it, already present a study not only of a man alone, but also of one who has deliberately chosen his alienation and constructed its physical simulacrum within which to emotionally incarcerate himself. It is difficult to imagine he had reserves of affection, or even attention, for Emiko. That she chose to indulge her need, or her desire, for Ogata in the absence of demonstrative love from him is made that much clearer by Honda's exposition of how Serizawa lives.

Whatever the stock representation of the laboratory recluse has been in science fiction filmography, Serizawa is assuredly not a mad scientist. As depicted in the original version of the film he appears to be a sober, focused, principled researcher who has earned his reputation among his colleagues through hard work and sheer brilliance, and surely, given how much stock the Japanese set by courage, by his wartime sacrifice. Mark Anderson describes him as "more ethically engaged and concerned for others than the implicitly negligent U.S. scientists who unleased the A-bomb and the H-bomb upon humanity in general and Japan in particular" (25).

In Shigeru Kayama's "G Project" story, Serizawa is 42 years old (Brothers, *Atomic Dreams* 27), and as played by Akihiko Hirata he appears at or near that age even though Honda and Murata supposedly rewrote his part to make him 27. The problem is that would have made him a teenager during the war, surely not a scientist. It also would create a host of other interpretive inconsistencies for the film's narrative arc, not the least of which is how he went from being a battle scarred youngster to an eminent scientist with an obviously well-funded laboratory during a nine year period when Japan was emerging from devastation and universities lay in ruins. In any case his wartime injury has scarred his face and his private concerns have engraved it with worry lines.

Aws Takashi Shimura's face hefts the pervasive sadness of *Gojira;* Hirata's narrower face, heavy eyebrows, and deeply etched worry lines convey the anguish of wartime fear, the disillusionment consequent of defeat, and the weight of carrying terrible secrets. Taken together, his age seems to remain Kayama's original 42 or thereabouts. He would thence be around 20 years older than his betrothed, Emiko, whom Kayama describes as 22 years old at the time of the story (*Ibid.*). Aside from emphasizing the involuntary nature of their betrothal, the age difference also positions them, temporally speaking, on opposite sides of the late war. This makes for more than a merely generational disparity. Since he had grown up when suicide was still a matter of honor in a way it no longer was post-occupation, his metaphorical *seppuku* is a self-justifying ritual which makes perfect if grisly sense.

Nonetheless, judging by the grief-stricken reactions of the crew and passengers of the Japan Coast Guard ship from which he had descended with his weapon, by 1954 there was no longer much glory in self-immolation. There is only a sense of tragic loss. He may be a martyr to a renewed, post–Humanity Declaration (*Ningen sengen*) emperor. Under pressure from General MacArthur, and in partial fulfilment of the terms of Japan's surrender, Emperor Hirohito presumably disavowed his status as a living god. Scholars quarrel over some of the terms Hirohito and his rescript author chose for his disavowal (an extended discussion of the verbal sleight-of-hand can be found here: http://www.ageekinjapan.com/humanity-declaration-人間宣言-ningen-sengen/). This declaration also diminished the stature which could be achieved by dying in the divine emperor's name. During the Pacific War, though, loss of life in service to the emperor, especially by suicide, was valorized by the nation's militaristic ethos. Even following the carnage of over 100,000 lives in the Tokyo fire raids of 1945, a toll exacted again in both atomic attacks, Japanese military leaders continued to speak of "the glorious death of the hundred million" (Murray and Millett 520), a mass self-immolation of the nation's entire population, if the allies invaded and conquered the homeland.

Gojira, set nine years later, shows us a very different sensibility. Its depiction of the monster's Tokyo rampage is full of scenes of fleeing Japanese trying desperately to save their bodies from being trampled or incinerated. Serizawa's suicide must be understood in this context. In Japanese terms, the heroic ethos of sacrifice, in retrospect, is now marked not merely as loss but as *waste*. As Anderson further notes, "in Gojira the loss of life is very clearly experienced as wrenching trauma, as grief to be ritually recognized and mourned by the nation" (28).

Honda is keen to make death look different than it did to a

III. Dramatis Personae

militarized Japan, but then he had never been taken in by that brutal mindset. His unblinking depiction of the suffering of Tokyo's citizens in the wake of Gojira's rampage, with its scenes of casualties flooding overwhelmed hospitals, burn victims trying to comfort each other, children watching their parents die, has nothing of the glorious about it. Its tragic pathos is instrumental in pushing Emiko past her emotional breaking point and forging her resolve to betray Serizawa's terrifying secret. Again, as Anderson has observed, "[Serizawa] is a martyr to modernity and to a Japan that identifies with universal humanism, but who also recognizes the pathological limitation of modernity. He recognizes that he is of modernity, but that modernity is pathological" (32).

Aside from his laboratory, which from our contemporaneous catbird seat looks like a model of steampunk futurism, he also, crucially, owns a television. This is significant because broadcast networks had only premiered in Japan a year earlier. Despite also owning a television, the Yamane household still features a radio from which it receives its most important information, not least of which are repeated notices of Gojira's emergence from Tokyo Bay. It is as if the radio symbolizes the old Japan, with its air raid warnings and militaristic propaganda, while the TV represents the new social order, "pathological" though it may be. The habit of TV viewing hadn't taken hold yet but the national broadcast of schoolgirls singing Akira Ifukube's haunting prayer for peace is what convinces the scientist to abandon his obstinate refusal to use his weapon against the destructive creature. There is a sense of transition being imparted.

Ultimately Serizawa who, as a veteran, straddles the psychological and historical divide between wartime and postwar Japan, enacts a suicide which paradoxically resolves the moral conundrum between those points of view. Serizawa avers he did not go looking for a super weapon but stumbled across it while conducting his research, and claims he was horrified by what he found. In this he mirrors J. Robert Oppenheimer's apologia for doing much of the theoretical work behind the American atomic bomb. ""It is a profound and necessary truth that the deep things in science are not found because they are useful; they are found because it was possible to find them" (qtd. in Rhodes 22).

Representing himself as a pacifist, he refuses to glory in his discovery even if he does have a blind spot about his unique responsibility to put a stop to Gojira. This is the conventional view of Serizawa most critics have taken, but I think this reading has been influenced by the way the American version was edited. In the original, after Hagiwara leaves, having gotten nowhere with his interview of the scientist, Emiko leads up to her confession she is breaking off their engagement by asking about his research. Serizawa then asks Emiko if she wants to see what he's up to. Taken aback only slightly, Emiko consents.

In the American version, Hagiwara's entire interview scene is deleted. Emiko arrives at her fiancé's home and says there is something important she must tell him. Serizawa, appearing to anticipate her announcement she is ending their engagement, cuts her off by saying "but there is something far more important which I must show you." He then takes her downstairs to his laboratory and demonstrates something which frightens and disgusts her. We don't get to see what it is yet, but we know it was awful.

Moreover this scene begs a few questions concerning Serizawa's own thoughts about their betrothal. He expresses little affection for her, except for cradling her for a very few moments when she is shattered by the horror in his aquarium. Otherwise, he seems, if not aloof, at least more preoccupied with his research than with her. When Hagiwara leaves his home and she asks him what he's been up to, it's apparent they don't spend much time together and he doesn't confide much about his work to her either. That he chooses this moment when Hagiwara has cracked his shell of privacy to take her into his confidence, after they have likely been engaged since her childhood, is more indicative of how disturbing the journalist's awareness of his work must seem to him than it is of his intimacy with her. In less complicated circumstances it might even have been a relief.

His suicide at film's end thus becomes even more of a conundrum: yes, his determination to bury his discovery along with himself is one aspect of it, but, again, as a transitional figure from a more tradition-bound ethos the formal humiliation of her apostasy, as opposed to mere heartbreak, also bears upon it.

In Honda's original, Serizawa is a more problematical figure than has been generally remarked by the film's critics. He is not a milquetoast intellectual. Rather, he is a toughened veteran of a brutal war, and he is also physically powerful. In his struggle with Ogata over the lockbox containing the oxygen destroyer, he knocks the younger man to the floor where Ogata bangs his head against the furniture and opens

III. Dramatis Personae

a wound. This episode foreshadows Serizawa's impending assumption of his mythic role as monster slayer. According to Foster, in the *Nihon Shoki*, an ancient compilation of Japanese lore, Susa-no-O's slaying of the great dragon *Yamata no Orochi* is an early example of what would come to be known as a *yōkai taiji*, a traditional narrative in which a hero manages to vanquish or kill a dangerous spirit or monster (*The Book of Yōkai* 35). As he watches Emiko dress the bleeding cut in her lover's head, he doubtless realizes her affections have shifted away from him for good. It is as if this realization, especially after listening to the televised schoolgirls' prayer for deliverance, frees him to change his mind and assume his heroic persona.

Serizawa's lost eye is another feature which can be read several ways. Certainly, on one level it is his badge of suffering and evidence he has experienced more than enough brutality. In this sense it functions as a justification for his pacifism. It could also be regarded as another aspect of Honda's use of chiaroscuro, with Serizawa's black hair and eyepatch contrast with his pasty complexion, like an analogue of the good and evil impulses warring within him. Although I wouldn't suggest Honda or Murata intended to incorporate Vodoun symbolism, the eyepatch covering his right orbit reminds me of a story mythologist Joseph Campbell told about the Haitian *lwa* Ghede Nibo, a lord of the netherworld. When asked why he wears the prosthesis Ghede replies "with this [left] eye I see the world; with this [right] eye I see within" (personal communication).

This aphorism suits Dr. Serizawa well. While Yamane and the others stand beside the harbor and watch Gojira leave an apocalyptic scene behind, Serizawa sits in his laboratory impassively watching Tokyo burn on his TV set. It takes Ogata's insistence and the fortuitous intervention of a televised high school girls' choir to make his decision to use the weapon inevitable. In this regard, Serizawa's lost eye can be viewed as symbolic of a moral blind spot.

I must not fail to mention the journalist Hagiwara, who is important to the story's resolution but who doesn't receive a lot of critical attention. As played by veteran character actor Sachio Sakai, he could charm the curlers off Medusa. Hagiwara is a lens through whose eyes we make new discoveries about Gojira as well as about some of the film's significant characters. He has much in common with folkloric Japanese trickster figures like *Kitsuni* or *Tanuki*, or especially, given his eventual

In Search of Godzilla

role in defeating our particular dragon, Susa-no-o. Of this, we will have much more to say later. He is ubiquitous and he is an instigator. According to Robert Ellwood, tricksters in Japanese myth defy boundaries and bring order to chaotic situations (142–143). Hagiwara meets all these qualifications. He shows up everywhere, at security briefings, on Odo Island, as a Diet committee witness, in the halls of the security offices bearding disgruntled fishing executives. He has no compunction about bursting into Ogata's office to disrupt a private moment between the sailor and Emiko. Moreover, he catalyzes a sequence of events leading up to Serizawa's decision to use his oxygen destroyer against Gojira as well as inadvertently forcing resolution to the film's otherwise insoluble romantic triangle, even if it is a tragic one.

We first encounter him at the Coast Guard office reporting by phone the string of ship disasters to his editor. We next see him on Odo Island when he disembarks from a helicopter sent by the government to talk to the natives about the mysterious disasters occurring off their coast. Masaji, Shinkichi's star-crossed brother, insists in response to Hagiwara's questions there's a monster prowling the local seabed. Hagiwara's skepticism infuriates him. That same evening, as he attends the islanders' *kagura* expiation ceremony, the reporter asks Izuma, a local elder whose very name identifies him as an elemental extension of the Izu Archipelago to which Odo belongs, to explain the island's tradition of their sea monster.

During his conversation with Izuma he elicits the first mention of the monster's name. "Gojira, huh?" he repeats thoughtfully. We next see him both covering and testifying before the Diet committee which reviews the damage claims of the islanders following Gojira's nocturnal march across Odo. He looks a bit embarrassed as he tells the audience whatever caused the damage crushed the houses and helicopter from above. Wangling a spot with Yamane's subsequent research party, he prowls the disaster site with his camera and once again pops up everywhere; he is among the first to the top of Hachiman Hill to witness the monster's initial appearance.

My favorite Hagiwara moment occurs while he covers Dr. Yamane's report to the Diet committee some days later. When the committee members erupt in acrimony over Yamane's revelation that Gojira was loosed on the world by H-bomb testing, Hagiwara stands behind Yamane, Tanabe, and the other witnesses. They look grim and even

III. Dramatis Personae

sad, if not embarrassed, at the unfolding spectacle of dissension. Our reporter, who has likely covered the Diet's raucous meetings before, barely suppresses a mischievous smile. He's going to dine out on what's happening in that committee room and grins like a kid in a candy store about it. Not a bad attitude at all, especially when you've just had Gojira snarling in your face.

A day or so later, as the security officials announce their decision to attack the monster with depth charges, Hagiwara sits just to the minister's right, taking down notes. After the bombardment fails and Gojira surfaces for the first time in Tokyo Bay, we see the journalist interviewing irate fishing company executives in the security headquarters hallway. Then, just before his editor sends him to interview Serizawa, he sits in his office, with commuter trains passing behind him—foreshadowing Gojira's destruction of the Shinagawa rail yard—discussing with colleagues the pros and cons of killing the monster versus the cost of allowing it to live so it can be studied. "Right, it's a complicated question," he says. Complicated indeed.

Most significantly, it is Hagiwara who brings Emiko with him to his meeting with Serizawa, setting up the scientist's revelation to her of his oxygen destroyer as well as stumbling upon something darker about our scientist. Hagiwara's interview is a pivotal moment in the film, for its characters as well as for us as viewers. Our reporter's disclosure that a German scientist knows something about Serizawa's work, including that it might be useful against Gojira, provokes an irritated denial from Serizawa. "I don't know any German scientists," he protests, highlighting Japanese discomfort, even ten years later, about their old Axis alliance. The war with the west lingers evilly in the background of Japanese culture throughout the postwar period. It was part of the ethos for years afterward and *Gojira* was not the only creative project to address this matter of war guilt. At approximately the same time, novelist Shūsaku Endō was composing *The Sea and Poison*, a harrowing story about criminal medical experiments urged upon Japanese doctors by the military. His book would be published in 1957, three years after *Gojira* and two after *Record of a Living Being*.

That his revelatory exchange with Hagiwara renders Serizawa the fulcrum of this matter of residual war guilt is an important dimension of the film. The entire subject has been a late addition to the growing body of Godzilla criticism, which, I think, is a positive development.

In Search of Godzilla

Insofar as it demonstrates how profound Honda's vision actually is, it further validates our critical efforts. An aspect of this evolving discussion concerns how much of an expiation, or how much of an avoidance, of that guilt this film represents. Serizawa's wartime activities raise the specter of Japanese responsibility for the war and disprove assertions of critics like Rhoads and McCorkle, who cite Anne Allison. They find *Gojira* an effort to hold Japan blameless and pin all blame on the U.S. for the atomic attacks on its cities. Allison writes, "[Godzilla] signifies WWII as a travesty of nature brought on by the atomic blasts of the Americans. For Japanese audiences, then, [Godzilla] provided a vehicle for reliving the terror of war relieved of any guilt or responsibility— solely, that is, from the perspective of victim" (45).

Another American critic, Susan Napier, viewed *Gojira* as an exemplar of both "nuclear anxiety and easy moral certainties" (331). Remembering that *Gojira* was made for its domestic audience, I would argue, rather, that in the person of Serizawa the film quite reasonably raises the specter of Japanese responsibility and holds it before its spectators, daring them to look away. Its "moral certainties," in the forms of Serizawa's compromised pacifism and Yamane's moral myopia, are hardly "easy." Honda and Murata subject both of them to difficult processes of self-interrogation.

Hagiwara's assertion reveals Serizawa may indeed have shared information about his project with at least one former Axis colleague, for how else would it have led back specifically to him? We're left to ponder the circumstances of his conversation with the German. Was it during or after the war? Is Serizawa's pacifism so acute because he now has misgivings about having been part of the Japanese war effort or cooperated with the Nazis?

Although Kalat argues "it would be a considerable stretch" to assume he has worked with Japan's axis allies (68), I don't think it would be. First, Honda didn't put much of anything in his film gratuitously. Second, we're not told anything about Serizawa's wartime activities but it is unlikely Japan, which had several active secret scientific and wartime atomic programs of its own (see Wilcox, *Japan's Secret War*, and Charles River Editors, *The Axis Powers' Nuclear Weapons Program*), among them the army's Project Ni-Go and the Navy's project F-Go, would waste a talented scientist on the frontline trenches. Serizawa, a chemist, would have been especially useful to the Japanese atomic

III. Dramatis Personae

projects as well as their programs to develop synthetic gasoline, fertilizer, and aviation fuel.

The Japanese also ran a criminal medical experiments program (see Sigmund Shen 95–96). Shiro Ishi was Surgeon General of the Japanese Army. He was in charge of the notorious Unit 731, or the Manshu Detachment. Granted immunity from war crimes prosecution in return for testimony about his experiments, he oversaw the vivisection of war prisoners and helped to develop poison gasses. As mentioned above, the repressed issue of Japanese medical war crimes was finally covered in *The Sea and Poison* by novelist Shūsaku Endō (1957) and made into a film directed by Kei Kumai in 1986. Nothing *Gojira* discloses about Serizawa's wartime work, however, suggests that he had anything to do with Unit 731.

As fanciful as the notion of an oxygen destroyer was for its time, it was predicated by hypothetical work on both industrial and atomic weapons development. Where would such an idea have come from? Another of *Gojira*'s many layered ironies is that the process rendering ordinary water into deuterium, or heavy water, an isotope vital to moderating chain reactions, uses electrolysis to crack water molecules to isolate hydrogen from oxygen. Serizawa's oxygen destroyer would, in effect, amplify the process of making deuterium. In his apologia about how he found the chemical reaction at the heart of his troubling discovery, he explains to Emiko his desire "to study oxygen from every angle." A crucial step in enriching uranium for atomic weapons, the process of heavy water electrolysis was also industrial—a key to enriching fertilizer, for example—and was not a military secret. Even so, Japanese physicists were actually ahead of the West in their conviction that deuterium could be useful in enriching uranium, controlling fission, and using hydrogen to enhance the explosive force of fission bombs:

> Enrico Fermi and Edward Teller were not, however, the first to conceive of using a nuclear chain reaction to initiate a thermonuclear reaction in hydrogen. That distinction apparently belongs to Japanese physicist Tokutaro Hagiwara of the faculty of science of the University of Kyoto. Hagiwara had followed world fission research and had conducted studies of his own. In May 1941 he lectured on "Super-explosive U235," reviewing existing knowledge [Rhodes 550].

Any chemists involved with heavy water production would have fully to understand the properties of oxygen because the production of

In Search of Godzilla

deuterium requires eliminating heavier isotopes of oxygen and lighter hydrogen to facilitate the electrolytic reaction by which the hydrogen isotope D20 is created, in effect dismantling or "destroying" oxygen (Wilcox 114). Fraught with limitations on funding and technology, bedeviled by rivalries between its military services, Japan abandoned uranium enrichment processes dependent on deuterium by early 1943 (Pacific War Historical Society 34–36). A young chemist like Serizawa who had been working on any of the Japanese nuclear weapons or propulsion projects would then have been freed to study oxygen or at least to contemplate what he had already learned through his earlier work.

And though heavy water has a range of other important chemical and industrial applications, and though a talented chemist would have been seconded to another wartime project like the manufacture of fertilizer and synthetic fuels, *Gojira* is based on overarching anti-nuclear themes. These themes ought to contextualize properly how the tormented scientist's wartime work might have led him to the oxygen destroyer. Serizawa's discovery seems eerily like a natural extension of research he might have performed on one phase of the aborted Japanese atomic weapons project. It might also explain why, in his anguished defense of his refusal to deploy his weapon, he equates it so readily with nuclear bombs.

There is a bitter irony in all this. Though usually described as an anti-nuclear metaphor, Serizawa's super weapon could also be taken as a consolation prize for the failure of Japanese military science to construct and deploy an atomic bomb. In effect, it is backhanded compensation. Surely in the audience for *Gojira* there were embittered survivors of the Pacific War, which must have seemed futile in retrospect, who took vicarious satisfaction from the idea of a homegrown super weapon. This was a movie of many catharses at the time of its theatrical release. Though surely not intentional on the pacifistic Honda's part the oxygen destroyer, perceived as redemption for imperial Japan's failed atomic program, is one more of them.

Another interesting coincidence is that the right side of Serizawa's face, behind and beside his eyepatch, shows unmistakable burn scarring. When Ogata opines Serizawa lost his eye during the war, he doesn't tell us how, and I believe that ambiguity is deliberate. It needn't have been incurred on the front lines. Industrial complexes where chemical work was being done were regular targets of American bombs. RIKEN,

III. Dramatis Personae

Japan's leading atomic laboratory just outside of Tokyo, was destroyed by American B-29s in an incendiary raid on March 9–10, 1945 (Charles River Editors 76–77).

Speaking of RIKEN, one of the problems Japanese physicists had to overcome in their ultimately failed efforts to weaponize uranium was the corrosivity of uranium hexafluoride gas, the manufacture of which was an intermediate step in the isolation of the U-235 isotope needed to create an atomic explosion. The gas constantly ate away at the tubes of the separation units being used to process it (Wilcox 153, 416). Gojira's atomic breath is not fire but a corrosive radioactive aerosol. Its similarity to uranium hexafluoride deepens the monster's identification with atomic weaponry.

Adding yet another level of irony to the story, the scientist's mention of his own weapon in the context of nuclear and thermonuclear bombs is consistent with what we know about the Manhattan Project's scientists and engineers in their fears about how uncontrollable a chain reaction involving hydrogen might be, as any scientist contemplating a weapon using water as a catalyst would have to have:

> [Edward] Teller offered several [reactions] which a fission bomb or a Super might inadvertently trigger. He proposed to the assembled luminaries the possibility that their bombs might ignite the earth's oceans or its atmosphere and burn up the world, the very result Hitler occasionally joked about with Albert Speer.... Was there really any chance that an atomic bomb would trigger the explosion of the nitrogen in the atmosphere or the hydrogen in the ocean? This would be the ultimate catastrophe [Rhodes 614].

All of this may be speculative but Honda has placed clues and hints before us which I don't believe are accidental. Several prominent Japanese scientists, like atomic program leader Yushio Nishina, had written and published newspaper accounts of their involvement in military projects as early as 1946 (Wilcox 285). Given his desire to "make radiation visible" in the form of Gojira, it is not unlikely that an artist as fastidious as Honda would have researched such matters. He, Murata, and Kayama certainly had more than enough time to read these accounts, many of which were publicly available, before refining Serizawa's character and imagining his history. Most critics concur that he is the most complicated of Honda's creations, but on closer regard just *how* complicated he is, and how much of the troubled history of Japanese science he represents, becomes more apparent.

In Search of Godzilla

I credit the director with setting up Hagiwara's interview precisely to raise the question of his most intriguing character's wartime activities. A multi-purpose vignette, it prepares his audience for the revelation of the chemist's weapon as well as hints at the hitherto unguessed complexities of Serizawa's history. Germany and Japan were allies and nine years later Serizawa is still touchy about the mention of German colleagues. In lieu of this his work takes on a guilty aspect. It adds resonance and background depth to the anguish he displays in his confrontation with Emiko and Ogata. Furthermore, the potential collaboration scenario is consistent with the film's theme of irresponsible applications of science. "A-bombs against A-bombs. H-bombs against H-bombs," he protests. "As a scientist, no, as a human being, adding another terrifying weapon to humanity's arsenal is something I cannot allow." Perhaps most tellingly, as Emiko walks Hagiwara to the door we see Serizawa looking profoundly disturbed. The reporter's revelation has clearly struck a deep, unnerving chord.

It is instructive to note that around the turn of the century the Meiji government actively encouraged European professors to come to Japan and to lecture in their own language to encourage Japanese students to become multilingual. One of the languages Japanese students were urged to learn was, of course, German. It was the tongue in which much advanced work was being done in the sciences (Gordon 192). In the later interwar period the emphasis, in tune with the political climate, was even more heavily on German. As a young chemist, Serizawa would very likely have studied, and been familiar with, the language and studied German texts and journals. However, the Japanese were also closely following American science insofar as they could access it before Pearl Harbor. Serizawa seems to have studied English because he calls his discovery the "okishijin desutoroiyā," an English cognate rather than, say, *Sauerstoffzerstörer*.

The Nazis closely restricted where their scientists and engineers were permitted to travel, which restricted fruitful exchanges of ideas and interdicted the progress of German science during the Third Reich. However, it also made their scientific community more hermetic, or pressurized. Even so, dialogue with Italian and Japanese was more loosely permitted as a matter of Axis privilege. Aside from journals, which were fewer in number and limited in distribution much like the travels of their contributors, "Scientists also communicate with

III. Dramatis Personae

colleagues, mediated through oral and written communication" (Gordon 189). Therefor Serizawa, even as a graduate student, would in the interwar years have had access to the work of German chemists who also would have had access to his. Postwar the stature of German science was reduced, and punitive restrictions on dialogue between most western powers and the defeated nation were in effect for a time (Gordon 212). Any number of German scientists simply published or went to conferences in neutral Switzerland to circumvent the restrictions. The Japanese, postwar, while widening their access to western science, also hung onto their old channels of communication and influence.

From Sigmund Shen's point of view, "Serizawa forces [Emiko] to witness this painful demonstration [of the oxygen destroyer] ... as if he needs her to help carry the burden of his knowledge of both the terror of what he has made, and his refusal to end the destruction of his nation" (97). But the timing of his decision to show it to her suggests even more complicated motives. Is he perhaps re-enacting a self-redemptive psychodrama by swearing Emiko to secrecy because he regrets ever having discussed his work with others? Given this possibility, it is almost as if he is atoning *via negativa* for his earlier career. As Ryfle and Godziszewski see it, "Serizawa is inherently good.... [he] has been likened to physicist J. Robert Oppenheimer, father of the atomic bomb, who came to fear that the forces he had helped to unleash might bring about the end of the world" (99). He's not happy word of his research could have traveled from Switzerland to a Tokyo newspaper.

Because of Hagiwara's intercession we do know this: when Serizawa tells Emiko he has never spoken of his discovery with anyone else, he is either lying to her or has withdrawn into denial. In effect, Hagiwara is our Bakhtinian "excess of seeing and knowing" who exposes for us how much more complicated Serizawa is than we realized, and how many other issues may be involved, not only in his decision to tell Emiko about his work, but in his decision to end his own life in the final moments of the film.

Serizawa surmounts his fear that his discovery "should fall into the wrong hands" because of a televised prayer service entitled "O Peace, O Light, Return." Composed for the film by Akira Ifukube, with libretto by Shigeru Kayama, the prayer is represented as a traditional hymn. Its title implies the battle against Gojira is a form of warfare and reminds us that the full name of the original version of the film is *Gojira King of*

Monsters, Record of Great Battles. Gojira, then, allegorically hefts upon his serrated back the detritus of the Bushido code and its modernist descendant, the militarism of the prewar and wartime Shōwa era. The broadcast juxtaposes images of crowded hospitals where refugees comfort one another with pans of the Hiroshima-like ruins of Tokyo.

The mise-en-scène broadens to reveal crowds of people, clad in traditional robes, holding prayer beads in Buddhist supplicative poses (which also resemble photos of Japanese listening to Hirohito's surrender rescript), listening to the broadcast as are Serizawa, Ogata, and Emiko in Serizawa's basement laboratory. Several critics have criticized this scene because the television set just "goes on," but I don't think the so called gaffe matters very much.

In 1954 television was still an emerging medium in Japan and wasn't running on anything like a 24-hour basis. Temporary blackouts make sense because the conurbation where the local stations were located had just been incinerated and Gojira had chewed through a broadcasting tower. Most households still got their broadcast news from radio; as we noted earlier, Serizawa's TV is one of only two in the film, the other being in the Yamane household. These two sets both belong to financially well off scientists, not salaried householders. Like the radio also in Yamane's parlor, where a sudden report Gojira has been sighted moving through the bay breaks silence, it may simply have been left on in case anything newsworthy occurred.

Nor can we overlook how—given his subsequent realization of Emiko's dual betrayal—his suicide may also be in part a response to his humiliation. Now, with Hagiwara as catalyst, national and personal defeat, cultural disintegration, and the specters of superweapon apocalypse all pile up on Serizawa's head. The inevitability of revealing his discovery to the world is the final blow. These pressures become each other's objective correlatives in *Gojira* with Serizawa as their dramatic fulcrum.

Fissures in the Traditional Family: The Yamanes

Aside from its religious and mythological allusions, the human drama of *Gojira*, like that of its alter ego *Record of a Living Being*, is grounded in disintegrating forms of family and social relations. In this

III. Dramatis Personae

sense Gojira is as much a product of the Taisho period, when Japan's westernization began in earnest, as he is of the Jurassic era. The narrative constructs Dr. Yamane as a *scientific* traditionalist. He is as rooted in an empiricist ethos as blinkered and amoral in its way as that of any nuclear physicist. Yamane is frustrated by the military's insistence on destroying the animal instead of conducting research into how it has survived the hydrogen bomb tests that have driven it to the surface. As if to emphasize his relation to an irrecoverable past, the elderly scientist bolts from his dining room in despair after watching televised coverage of the naval bombardment of the submerged monster, retreating to his study where he is posed with his back to the camera and to the modern audience—sitting in darkness, with a facsimile Stegosaurus skeleton on the desk to his left.

Honda, as always, knows exactly what he's doing in the composition of this frame. Yamane's proximity to the skeleton emphasizes his link to the ancient past and to tradition, including the hospitality Ogata shortly thereafter violates when the young sailor insists the government is correct in trying to kill Gojira. His impertinence only earns his would-be father-in-law's ire. The ersatz fossil with its smoothly ellipsoid dorsal plates, meanwhile, implicitly contrasts with the creature's jagged back. As the monster disintegrates at the bottom of Tokyo Bay under the impact of Serizawa's oxygen destroyer, he becomes a ghostly simulacrum of the skeleton on Yamane's desk. This constellation of symbols is another reference to a world as lost as the traditional Japan of art and ritual, just as Gojira personifies a world—both paleontological and mythological—that *refuses* to go gently into its own good night.

Contrasts and tension between traditional and modern Japan run crucially through the film's human characters, notably in the odd romantic triangle between Emiko, Ogata and Serizawa. What makes it odd isn't the mere fact of a triangle—the "usual triangle," as Steve Martin comments in the American redaction. Unanswered questions about it, especially how it nests in the context of the Yamane household, make it odd. We're not told much about how or when the daughter of a patrician academic like Dr. Yamane got together with a marine salvage diver. Emiko has not yet formally broken her youthful engagement to Serizawa as the film's narrative begins. Nonetheless her affair with Ogata disregards the betrothal her father and, presumably, Serizawa's father had arranged for them as adolescents or teenagers. Since both Emiko and

In Search of Godzilla

Ogata have come of age in postwar Japan, when traditional social customs were in disarray, this should not be wholly surprising. It was a time when *ren'ai*, or romantic love, was gradually taking precedence over *omiai*, or prescriptive marriage.

Even so, the timeline of the romantic subplot is problematical. In the Transworld version of the film, Steve Martin comments, "The last time I had seen Emiko she had just become engaged to Dr. Serizawa," which is a puzzling remark. Martin refers to Serizawa as an "old college friend," which given their current ages must mean they knew each other before the war. We aren't told if they had seen each other since, or whether Martin's social visit to Tokyo was a reunion of sorts. I would venture, though, that because the Occupation ethos militated against old-school practices like forced betrothals, and because we do know that Serizawa was off soldiering in some capacity during the conflict, their engagement must have been arranged before the war, when they were both younger by fifteen years, or more.

Even though Ogata at one point reassures her "We have done nothing of which we should be ashamed," bringing Ogata into her father's house flaunts her defiance of traditional marriage customs. In the second scene of the film, directly following the Eiko-Maru disaster, we see Ogata in his apartment, emerging half-dressed and still toweling himself off from a shower while Emiko waits in the background, making plain that the two are lovers. When we next see them together, they are departing aboard a research vessel to study the unexplained destruction on Odo Island, standing together at the railing while Serizawa, standing on the pier, gazes up at them.

In the next scene, Ogata tells Emiko he was surprised to see Serizawa at the pier, indicating he knew who he was. Curious. Again, we know very little about the social circles within which the reclusive Serizawa and the ebullient Ogata might have become familiar with each other. Ogata then squints through a rangefinder, as if to mimic Serizawa's trademark lost eye or eye-patch and to establish some metaphorical relation between the two men, perhaps some shared moral shortsightedness. In a later scene, Ogata remarks on Serizawa's wound, as if he thought the loss of his eye was the reason Emiko no longer found him attractive. It is as if he is searching his conscience for some justification for their mutual bad faith. She reassures him that she had always regarded Serizawa as an older brother.

III. Dramatis Personae

What I find more interesting is how Ogata seems to be a fixture in the Yamane household, and we must assume either that Dr. Yamane is aware of the relationship and tolerates it, or that he is unaware of its true nature and regards Ogata as a family friend. In the latter scenario, Emiko and Ogata would both be showing *profound* disrespect to the elder Yamane by carrying on behind his back. Given the professor's steadfast conservatism in his commitment to his scientific ideas, this seems to me the more likely interpretation than that Yamane would merely wink at the defiance of the betrothal he had engineered.

The scenario is also complicated by the arrival of Shinkichi, a teenager from Odo Island whose brother and mother were killed by Gojira during his march through the village on the night of the mysterious gale. Ogata helps Shinkichi with his homework at the Yamane home, which indicates he and Emiko, or perhaps the elder Yamane, have adopted him. It is as if a shadow family has taken shape outside the traditional family, irrespective of Emiko's betrothal. Very curious, very heterodox.

That Serizawa understands what is going on between Emiko and Ogata is apparent in three separate scenes. In the first, we see Serizawa standing on the pier as Yamane's research team departs for Odo. He gazes impassively up at Emiko and Ogata on the deck of the ship, his expression a cipher. Emiko, on the other hand, smiles and waves at him as if nothing were wrong. Next, following her visit with Hagiwara, Emiko attempts to explain to him, privately, that she is breaking their engagement. However, the scientist sidetracks the conversation by offering to explain his research to her, cutting her off with some vehemence.

Emiko is so overcome by the demonstration of the oxygen destroyer that she drops the subject of her betrayal altogether, which we may guess is exactly what Serizawa wanted. He then makes her promise never to reveal what she has seen, fearing his destructive secret could be misapplied by political and military power-mongers. By imposing this oath, Serizawa also believes he can bind his fiancée closer to him amid his suspicion about her infidelity. Could we not read this as Serizawa's horror of disgrace trumping his concern about revealing his discovery, since by revealing his secret to his unfaithful betrothed, he sets in motion the ultimate disclosure to Ogata about the only weapon that could kill Gojira?

That disclosure is occasioned by the horror of Gojira's destruction of Tokyo. Working as a nurse's assistant in its aftermath, Emiko, devastated by the suffering all around her, suggests her identity with the ancient *kami* of compassion, Benten, about whom we will have more to say below. She takes Ogata aside and tells him what she knows about Serizawa's discovery. When they visit Serizawa to ask for the oxygen destroyer, the scientist is somber upon seeing them together. He appears to realize Emiko has come to end their betrothal, almost contemptuously acknowledging Ogata with "Oh, it's *you*," and, offering them seats at his parlor table.

Struggling to face the ordeal with some semblance of *noblesse oblige*, he is horrified when Ogata instead asks him for the weapon. Visibly stricken by her betrayal both of their engagement *and* of her promise never to discuss the oxygen destroyer, he glares at her accusingly. In an especially poignant vignette, he gazes sadly at his notes and blueprints as he feeds them to the fire, as though recalling the moments when each discovery first occurred to him. The look on his face and the spectacle of the burning notes together are too much for Emiko. Overcome with sadness and guilt she collapses in tears beside Serizawa's brazier.

The weapon itself is a shiny metallic globe encased within a glass and metallic cylinder. When Serizawa, who insists upon submerging with Ogata to place the weapon, opens the globe—which resembles the plutonium core of the "Fat Man" atomic bomb—using a trigger mechanism on the cylinder head, it initiates a vicious chemical chain reaction throughout Tokyo Harbor. After unleashing his weapon against the monster, Serizawa concludes the pattern of ameliorated sacrifice underpinning the entire film. He has secreted a knife in a pocket of his diving suit, which he wields like a *tanto*, the ritual dagger used in *seppuku*. He cuts the safety line and air hose which resemble entrails; Honda's camera focuses tellingly upon the blade slicing through the lines.

His suicide is an ambiguous act. Most commentators have interpreted it as fulfillment of his determination never to be coerced into revealing the secret of the oxygen destroyer. Surely, it is that, in part. Regardless, we overlook its continuity with the film's persistent allusions to unraveling codes of honor and respect if we do not also recognize it as his response to being dishonored by his fiancée. Within the mythic ethos of the story, we can also interpret his death as another

III. Dramatis Personae

ritual sacrifice to the ancient sea dragon *kami* Ryujin,* an ironic fulfillment of the Odo Island elder Izuma's insistence that the *kami* requires human blood. As Tsuda writes,

> The oldest record of [ritual sacrifice] is also in the *Nihon Shoki*. According to this, while the Emperor Jimmu, the founder of the Japanese Empire, was crossing the sea on his expedition to the east, a typhoon broke and his boat was soon adrift on the waves. Then Ina-ihi-no-mikoto, deploring the disposition of the deity, sacrificed his own body to the deity of the sea; thus the emperor could proceed.... There are many more traditions of this nature [763].

---

* For some general information on this, see, for example, M. Lindemans' entries on Ryujin at the *Encyclopedia Mythica* and at http://www.angelfire.com/falcon/ecsc-fwb/rj-md/DRAGON6.html.

IV

An American *Benshi* in Tokyo
Steve Martin

Hagiwara, as the original film's resident journalist, anticipates Raymond Burr's Steve Martin from the redacted American version, *Godzilla, King of the Monsters,* which was released in the United States two years after the original reached theaters in Japan. Throughout the war years Americans got their information and perspectives on Japan almost exclusively from journalists, including newsreels like Movietone which were staples of cinemagoing during and for years following the war. Insinuating a narrator who was a newspaperman into the imported filmic text of *Gojira* helped to maintain a sense of continuity, if not familiarity, with how domestic audiences experienced Japanese life. Even so, it may be Terry Morse, director of the Americanized version, thought two reporters were a bit much for one story. When Godzilla bites through that broadcasting tower and sends a dozen or so journalists plummeting to their deaths, the monster might be agreeing with him. It is ironic that at precisely this moment a crestfallen Steve Martin adds to his recorded report, "Nothing can save the city now."

The idea of a newspaperman narrating a monster movie wasn't novel. Arthur Conan Doyle's *The Lost World,* upon which the first dinosaur-on-the-loose movie was based, was narrated by reporter Ed Malone. Though deprived of voiceover privileges in that 1925 silent film epic, he remained a major character. In any event, international correspondent Martin nearly effaces the indigenous *shinbun* reporter altogether. Although he doesn't report to the original's audience as narratees, Hagiwara, as we have seen, catalytically discloses, or forces the disclosure, of several matters of importance and instigates the disclosures of others. Steve Martin's voiceover, on the other hand, addresses us directly. Taken together, Martin and his friend from an unspecified

IV. An American Benshi in Tokyo: Steve Martin

Japanese military or police agency, Tomo Iwanaga, assume the roles of *benshi*, the traditional offscreen narrators of silent films in Japan.

Beginning in the late 1800s with the earliest silent films, the *benshi* evolved as live interpreters of the action on screen. As theaters began showing longer, more narrative western films, another style of live interpretation, *kowairo setsumei*, developed. This style transcended mere explanation and included personal stylings and embellishments of the plot or commentary on the motivations of the characters (Dym). The film would be introduced by a solo *benshi* giving a plot synopsis and explanation of what the audience would be seeing; thence, other *benshi* standing in the wings of the theater would translate dialogue and offer real-time commentary about what was happening onscreen.

The impression created by a *kowairo setsumei* performance was that of a dubbed film in a time before dubbing occurred. The way Terry Morse edited *Godzilla, King of the Monsters* created an ironic matrix for the revivification of the *benshi*. Steve Martin supplies both introductory and narrative continuity as he introduces the film and partially explains what is going on while lying in the rubble of the press headquarters and, subsequently, while being treated for his injuries in a makeshift hospital. He also provides a brief history of the ship sinkings that precipitated the monster crisis. As the story progresses, he provides a running commentary as events unfold.

Only a few of the central characters in the Americanized *Godzilla* were dubbed, and even then not consistently. To make the film marketable in the United States, our American director had to find a way to translate much of the Japanese being spoken in it. Subtitling was out of the question; it was time consuming and unpopular with domestic audiences of the mid–1950s, who were feeling hegemonic about their language as well as their geopolitical status.

Such was the cultural climate in the United States that another factor in making *Godzilla* acceptable was the need to develop some sense of sympathy for, if not empathy with, the perpetrators of Pearl Harbor. Peter H. Brothers describes the American horizon of reception for Japanese cinema in the United States as Transworld prepped their redacted version for release and distribution:

> Outside of art-house critics and film buffs, even by the mid–1950s, very little was known about Japanese cinema, and even less was appreciated. For

In Search of Godzilla

many Americans the Japanese were still a reviled and distrusted people capable of any culpability (at the very least they were exotic, at the worst they were profoundly alien), and whatever they might be having a hand in ... they were incapable of creating anything substantive enough to warrant serious consideration. Kurosawa's *Rashomon* was the first Japanese film to open the eyes of foreigners in 1951 when it won the Gran Prix Prize at the Venice Film Festival, but over the intervening years very few Japanese films were widely known outside of their own country; even *Seven Samurai* and Kenji Mizoguchi's *Ugetsu* (*Ugetsu Monogotari*, 1953) had only limited distribution in America. Then came *Godzilla* [*Atomic Dreams* 165].

The crossover figure of security officer Tomo Iwanaga was ideal for encouraging a more cordial sensibility. Played by California-born Japanese-American actor Frank Iwanaga, who as a young man had spent time in Earl Warren's wartime concentration camps for American citizens of Japanese ancestry (Calisphere), Iwanaga spoke English without any foreign accent and formed a comfortable friendship with Raymond Burr's Steve Martin. The pair set an example of peaceful, even fond, coexistence. Despite Burr's often touchy-feely propensity to put his hands on his friend, which was not at all *de rigueur* among Japanese nor unique to Steve Martin—a character named Shigerioto, representing himself as an assistant to Serizawa, gets Martin's attention at the airport by tugging his sleeve—they appear to get along about as well as any American chums. This was a palliative gambit staged for domestic audiences, and it worked well. When Martin's rudimentary Japanese fails him, which is often, Iwanaga does the translating for him and for the audience.

Still, most of the Japanese characters in *Godzilla, King of the Monsters* are untranslated by dubbing or subtitling. Dr. Yamane speaks English in his two addresses to the Diet committee, in a brief conversation with Steve Martin in the hall outside the committee room, while measuring Godzilla's footprint on Odo Island, and while sulking in his office as the Japanese Coast Guard depth-charges Godzilla. Emiko and Ogata both speak English to Steve in the hospital, and to Serizawa in his laboratory and aboard the Coast Guard ship deploying the oxygen destroyer against the monster. Serizawa and Emiko speak English to each other during his demonstration of the oxygen destroyer in his laboratory. Serizawa's assistant Shigerioto and the burly cop at airport customs also speak English, but briefly. Otherwise, Japanese

IV. An American Benshi in Tokyo: Steve Martin

characters—even an American Japanese actor playing a frightened peasant on Odo Island—speak Japanese.

Tomo Iwanaga is the auxiliary or *kowairo setsumei benshi* who translates Japanese into English for Steve Martin and explains Odo Island lore to him. He assumes the redacted Hagiwara's function of translating Izuma's commentary and telling Martin, and us, the name of the island's folkloric sea monster during the Odo Island expiation ceremony, and later explains the plan to electrocute Godzilla with high tension wires if the monster tries to reach Tokyo again. Thereafter, he excuses himself to return to his station and disappears from the story, leaving the field to Martin as narrative monologuist. Henceforth, we will hear no more Japanese spoken. Ironically, inserted into the original as a white identity figure, Steve Martin as *benshi* renders the movie even more traditionally Japanese than the original.

Despite his English dialogues and monologues being subtitled in the later Japanese release of this version of the film in 1957, it was enough of a box office success that Toho henceforth incorporated its extended title, "King of the Monsters," into their future marketing of the Godzilla franchise (Kalat 59). If the Americanized version made modest headway in ameliorating the lingering animosities of Americans towards anything Japanese, it also scored points with its indigenous audience upon returning to Japan in this streamlined version.

Brothers cites the remarks of a Toho marketing executive, responding to the re-imported film's success: "The Japanese special effects were approved overseas and the [American] audience clearly appreciated them. With the release this time, we're hoping to gather fans who have not seen the film and have a liking for Western works. With the re-editing from the American side, it can be now enjoyed as much by adults" (*Atomic Dreams* 192–193). The presence of Frank Iwanaga, and his character's warm relationship with Steve Martin, was also heartening evidence that, at least, a cultural healing process had been set in motion by the unlikeliest of icons.

V

The Atomic Genie

So much has been written about the centrality of the atomic attacks on Japan and subsequent testing of hydrogen bombs in the South Pacific to the conception and substance of *Gojira* that it seems gratuitous to return to the topic here. However, the correlation between the nuclear threat and the creature is neither simple nor transparent. This has become especially true because the misleading sense of interregnum following the collapse of the Soviet Union has eroded over the second decade of the twenty-first century and finally evaporated with Russian strongman Vladimir Putin's repeated threats to use tactical nuclear warheads in his Ukraine misadventure. However, during that temporary lapse of concern, as Michael J. Blouin noted, "Godzilla as a monstrous icon sustains the vital purpose of continuing discussions surrounding atomic anxiety, once again refuting the certainty of any particular stance" (27).

The film, its monster, and the nuclear event are so inextricably joined on so many levels it is impossible to avoid further discussion. Nor has the topic been exhausted. Honda, Kayama, Murata and company made the atomic genie dance to many tunes. Fear of annihilation was only one of them. "A latex monster put forth by Toho Studios in 1954 is perhaps the 'nuclear text' par excellence," writes Blouin. "It developed into the face of nuclear destruction, an icon to encapsulate the breadth of the controversy, a signifier that struggles to touch upon the most unspeakable of moments" (86).

When the Soviet Union collapsed a lull in nuclear tensions followed it for a few all too brief decades, whereupon a theoretical window opened through which it became possible to re-evaluate the nuclear symbolism of the film. Even though the catastrophic meltdown of the Fukushima Daiichi reactors in 2011 was addressed more directly by 2016's *Shin Godzilla*, it nevertheless opened up a wider range of critical questions, even retrospectively, for the 1954 original.

V. The Atomic Genie

William Tsutsui has asserted that "Godzilla is a souvenir of our collective childhoods, an expression of an unrealizable desire to return to a simpler, gentler, less demanding era, to the sheltered security of youth" (210–211). Whereas this may well be true in the United States, the monster was surely not such a sentimental memory in Japan at the time of its 1954 release. Not coincidentally, Arthur C. Clarke's *Childhood's End* was published in 1954 as well. Its representation of Satan, or the alien being Karellan in whose image Satan had been fabricated by ancient civilization, like *Gojira*'s emergence closely following the dawn of the atomic age, was no coincidence either. The splitting of the atom represents, in both works, the very real end of our cultural childhood.

Westernization, with all its transformations of Japanese civilization, is generically symbolized in *Gojira* with the monster's radioactivity as its chassis. With the temporary retreat of the threat of global thermonuclear war we could see more clearly how anxiety about the technological threat also underpinned Honda's representation of Japanese spirituality and social conduct in decay. "Specters of modernity materialize in tropes of the fantastic, which actually run throughout science fiction and a number of other subgenres as well," writes Blouin (25). If the symbol of ancient Japan is Mount Fuji, the symbol of modern Japan was the Dai-Ichi Insurance Company building, General MacArthur's Tokyo headquarters. Within the discreet dystopia of *Gojira*, modernity may begin with the atomic bombings, but it takes flight with the makeover of Japanese culture by the allied occupation.

The Lucky Dragon Five episode* had occurred months earlier on *Gojira*'s narrative timeline. We know this because of the discussion by a trio of Tokyo rail commuters who mention "radioactive tuna." An episode which shook Japan's political and cultural life. It was one of producer Tomoyki Tanaka's motivators for making the film, and the disappearance of Odo Island's schools of fish doubtless reminded audiences of the nationwide tuna recall which followed the discovery that the ship's catch, already sold through the marketplace, was contaminated.

---

* See S. Galbraith, with F. Yukari and S. Atsushi, *Monsters Are Attacking Tokyo* (Los Angeles: Feral House, 1998), 215–16, for more details on the relevance of the Lucky Dragon Five incident to the making of *Gojira*. In the "commuter scene" wherein several salarymen and women compare the advent of Godzilla to the Tokyo fire raids and atomic bombings, the contaminated tuna from the ill-fated trawler is specifically mentioned.

In Search of Godzilla

The scandal likely accounted for Dr. Yamane's precautionary recruitment of his radiologist colleague Professor Tanabe for his research trip to Odo. Prior to that trip, no other connection had been made in the original film between the ship sinkings and radiation. In Japan, the connection was already so obvious it didn't have to be. In the American version, Steve Martin broaches the subject by noting the survivors of the sinkings suffered from "strange burns." Not until their investigation of the island's village do the researchers discover the contamination of the well and the monster's irradiated footprints.

Yamane uses this evidence, and the Strontium-90 in the sand from the trilobite he finds in Gojira's footprint, to link the beast to hydrogen bomb testing in the Marshall Islands. Prior to the Castle series of two H-bomb tests in the early 1950s, beginning in 1946 there had already been five tests of newer designs of atomic bombs there as well. Even though Yamane focuses on the H-bomb tests in his report to the Diet, Gojira's ecosystem had already taken a nuclear shellacking. Moreover, not only is his flesh scarred by the bombs' heat and radiation, but the creature carries his hands stiffly upraised like the *hibakusha*, survivors of the Hiroshima and Nagasaki bombings with their seared flesh, swollen joints, and palsied tendons. In this sense Gojira is a *hibakusha* himself.

Death, violent death, is neither optically sterilized nor eroticized in *Gojira*, as it often is in science fiction films of the 1950s and 1960s. However, it is usually collectivized. This is unsurprising given how much of its audience had experienced the repeated bombings and incinerations of Japanese communities during the Pacific War. Victims of lethal violence include Shinkichi's mother and brother on Odo Island; the fleeing Tokyo citizens roasted by the creature's atomic breath as they clamor for shelter; the occupants of a police car who can't get away from their vehicle before it's incinerated by the angry beast; a mother holding her children on a Tokyo sidewalk as burning buildings collapse around them; a child who watches her mother die in an overcrowded hospital surrounded by other victims of the monster's assault; railway passengers cowering under an upended coach Gojira soon crushes; and the television newsmen plummeting from their observation tower as the creature chews through it.

These fatalities are usually accompanied by cries of pain and terror. Honda, determined to communicate in the form of his monster

V. The Atomic Genie

the horrors of wartime violence to which he had been witness, pulls no punches. Susan Sontag identified the characteristically collective image of death that set in with the atomic bomb as

> the trauma suffered by everyone in the middle of the 20th century when it became clear that from now on, to the end of human history, every person would spend his individual life under the threat not only of individual death, which is certain, but under something almost insupportable psychologically—collective incineration and extinction which could come at any time, virtually without warning [223].

In *Gojira* everyone who dies, dies collectively except Serizawa, who makes the decision for himself—paradoxically asserting by intent his defiance of the anxiety of the collective destruction of man by nuclear war. Akira Kurosawa's companion piece to his friend Honda's film, *Record of a Living Being*, features the family of old Nakajima, who is obsessed with the nuclear threat. His children and in-laws use what they view as his irrationality as an excuse to get their hands on his fortune, keep him from leaving for the faux safety of Brazil, and preserve their own source of income. Emiko and Ogata, on the other hand, try to navigate the ramifications of the Gojira crisis in the process of uncottering her childhood betrothal to Serizawa.

In both cases the *pikadon*, the atomic fireball, looms hugely in the background. That fireball reappears in the antepenultimate scene of *Record* in the guise of the sun in a projection of Nakajima's nuclear paranoia. For Serizawa, the oxygen destroyer is also a simulacrum of the atomic attack; the skeletonized and vaporized fish in his aquarium are revisitations of the disintegrated or carbonized victims within the horrific two mile radii of the Hiroshima and Nagasaki explosions. It is hardly farfetched to speculate that when the anguished scientists tears at his own hair and exclaims "I wish I had never invented it," it is that fireball and its victims he envisions in his mind's eye.

The celebrated scene in *Gojira* of a mother gathering her young children together on a sidewalk while the conflagration around them intensifies, crying, "we'll be with Daddy soon," is another case in point. The scene is heartrending. Though many critics have assumed Daddy was killed "in the war," her children are far too young to have been conceived before 1945. Even so, the family tableau confabulated here by Honda practically duplicates a famous photo by Alfred Eisenstadt of a

In Search of Godzilla

mother and her child in the ruins of Hiroshima which appeared in a series by *Life* magazine during the several years following the war.[*] If this is not a direct reference to the atomic bombings or the fire raids, it is at least a metaphor for them however anachronistic its mise-en-scène. But it serves another, if less iconic than personal, function. What we see here is a distinctly individuating tragedy, a reminder that at the heart of any mass immolation are suffering individuals.

Dr. Yamane's solicitude for the opportunity he believes Gojira affords him cross-correlates with Serizawa's refusal to consider using his discovery against the monster. Yamane wants to understand how the beast survived the hydrogen bomb test that brought it to the surface, seething with radioactivity that should have killed it. In arguments with the military authorities and within his own family, especially with the upstart Ogata, he insists Gojira should not be destroyed but should be studied. In this sense Yamane regards Gojira, like the nuclear event itself, not as much as a concrete event but more like what Blouin has called "a nuclear text" to be explicated (86). The term "nuclear event" has come to mean rather more than the bombings of Hiroshima and Nagasaki. In scholarly and critical discussion, it stands for the bombings and the entire range of discursive approaches to them, and to the nuclear threat, in more inclusive terms.

In this, Honda and Murata anticipated how criticism of the nuclear menace would develop over the ensuing decades. As a representative of the waning years of the Taisho and onset of the Shōwa Periods of Japan, Yamane personifies the empirical study of supernatural phenomena which characterizes an era of modernization. He does not necessarily discount the uncanny but he would, as it were, "naturalize" the supernatural force which has been unleashed against Japan. It takes the fiery destruction of Tokyo to place before Yamane, as well as before his young *Doppelgänger* Serizawa, the human suffering to which both men's private concerns have blinded them. The two of them are linked by history, by fate, and by their empirical training.

However there is more. Yamane's moral blindness is mirrored by Serizawa's eye patch. For Yamane, radiation is the unnatural phenomenon

---

[*] See, for example, https://granarygallery.com/artist-item.php?itemId=3287468&title=Mother+and+Child+4+months+After+Atomic+Bomb%2C+Hiroshima+1946&artistId=196576&artist=Alfred+Eisenstaedt&fromCart=1.

V. The Atomic Genie

whose study transcends the obvious lethality of the monster. The younger scientist excuses his discovery of the frangibility of the oxygen atom by insisting he was acting "purely in the interests of science." Now, though, he is paralyzed by his fear that his oxygen destroyer might someday be deployed as a military option, of a chain reaction of disintegrating seas consuming all life in the water and, by extension—though this is only implicit in his description of how his creation works—destroying all oxygen-releasing algae therein. He understands what this would mean for life on Earth.

Serizawa has been compared by some critics to J. Robert Oppenheimer, the scientific director of the Manhattan Project, under whose aegis the atomic bomb was developed (see, for example, Kalat 50). In the most common interpretation of Serizawa's personality, this simile is only partially viable insofar as both men came to regret their discoveries.

As far as we know Serizawa did not go looking to devise a weapon although, as discussed, this is by no means certain. Oppenheimer guided the development and construction of the atomic bomb deliberately. Serizawa's reluctance to use the oxygen destroyer makes him an anomaly among the scientists who feature prominently in the science fiction films of the 1950s and '60s in his immediate realization of the danger of his discovery. No doubt this is due not only to his own experience of the brutality of war but to his belonging to a community on the receiving end of an atomic attack. His character would seem to have left no imprint on the writing of the scientist in succeeding films, who are anxious to use their discoveries to kill off whatever threat imperils civilization. These men have no compunctions about it. His natural heir, if he has one, would be Ian Malcolm, the mathematician in *Jurassic Park* played by Jeff Goldblum, who, confronted with Ingen's wholesale cloning of dinosaurs, warns that science is an "invasive" and "arrogant" mindset.

VI

The Mythic and Religious Gojira

MUCH AS ITS MANY SIGNIFIERS of older forms of culture in decline alert us to what the film's underlying concerns are, its persistent gestures towards ancient Japanese religious myths and rituals ironically disclose its cognizance of Japan's postwar social and spiritual transformation. These references not only depict how deeply the film's overmastering radiophobia has penetrated Japan's spiritual life. They also demonstrate how resilient Japanese legends, mythology, and spirituality remained after seven years of Occupation psychological and educational campaigns against them. While *Gojira* explored the modernization of its social order and the depredations of radiophobia, the nation's mythological unconscious occupied, even commandeered, those explorations. This reciprocal process adds yet another layer of irony to Honda's film.

Michael Dylan Foster is circumspect about equating Gojira too closely with the nation's imposing realm of the supernatural:

> To be sure, the difference between a kaiju and a yōkai is a murky one at best, but the relative invisibility of Gojira within the modern discourse on yōkai highlights the way yōkai came to be defined in postwar Japan. Does Gojira's fictional birth somehow set it apart from the yōkai we have been looking at? Is it different because of its genesis within the medium of popular cinema? [*Pandemonium and Parade* 160].

The distinction between yōkai's roots in history, tradition, and nostalgia, and Gojira's contemporary cinematic origins poses a range of interpretative problems, and Foster acknowledges Honda and his crew were probably aware of them. "As if in recognition of this, a backstory is created for Gojira in the film—he is a creature of local legend, emerging from the depths to fulfill his destiny" (161). While understanding

VI. The Mythic and Religious Gojira

that Foster's reservations are voiced in the interest of clarity, his ultimate rejection of Gojira as a yōkai because he is a dinosaur, not a composite being like most other yōkai, isn't entirely accurate. He is based on the platform of a Charles Night–era, tail-dragging Tyrannosaurus, with the arms of an Iguanodon, and his back is festooned with Stegosaurus dorsal plates, albeit they are tortured and jagged rather than ovoid. His physiological hybridity crosses millions of years, two geological epochs—the Jurassic and Cretaceous—and the ravages of nuclear exposure.

Further implicit in Foster's observation is the notion Godzilla's repeated alterations in sequel after sequel, over the years, carry him further and further beyond the scope of traditional historical and sociological folklore studies of yōkai. What is really carrying him away, as both Foster and Igarashi have noted, is not so much his ongoing cinematic transformations but the conveyor belt of history and fading markers of the Pacific War. As Brothers noted, though, "The idea of a typhoon heralding the monster's arrival was another unique cinematic convention and the concept of the creature being connected to a severe weather event—coming on the heels of a religious ritual specifically orchestrated to drive it away—bestowed upon it a supernatural characteristic which has never been revisited in any other Godzilla film" (472–473). Ergo Gojira remained entangled in the ancient lore of *Yamato* despite his expulsion from the abyss into a modernizing world.

Yet those historical and cultural changes were much of what the monster, holding those markers before him, was staged against.

Regardless, as the mythologist Joseph Campbell so forcefully reminds us, one cannot harness powerful archetypes out of the cultural unconscious without proliferating interpretations.* Myths are polysemous. They cut both ways, and then some. On New Year's Day of 1946, under pressure by the Supreme Commander of the allied occupation, Emperor Hirohito ostensibly put an end to the tradition of the emperor as an incarnate divinity in his so-called "Humanity Declaration" (*Ningen sengen*). The linguistic sleight-of-hand by which Hirohito maintained a tenuous link to the myth of his descent from the sun goddess

---

* See Campbell's introduction to *The Masks of God, Vol. I: Primitive Mythology* (New York: Viking, 1968).

In Search of Godzilla

Amaterasu (and by extension to Ryujin, Jimmu and the former's contemporary manifestation, Gojira) need not concern us here.

The exact wording of the declaration is still a matter of contention among linguists and historical scholars. Meanwhile, it is both ironic and amusing to note that while MacArthur forced Hirohito to shed his veneer of divinity, the marketing department of Toho Studios was restoring the "God" to Gojira, so that if the Showa emperor had divested his great mother, the film re-emphasized his relationship with great-grandaddy Ryujin.

However, Hirahito's declaration coincided with an ongoing campaign by the occupation to dismantle the so-called "State Shinto" apparatus through which nationalists and militarists had enforced their valorization of the Bushido* code and the Samurai spirit. Democratization of Japan, the allies believed, hinged on stripping away imperial mythology, and secularizing Japanese society. In this sense, Gojira as a re-emergent deity ironically, if not vengefully, forces the old myths back down the throat of a modernizing culture in a manner no longer suited to what it has become, and by means which are utterly destructive. The *kaiju / kami* objectifies, in addition to radiophobia, the national spirit deformed by defeat, westernization, and ancient traditions abandoned at gunpoint. This is the same impulse towards self-sacrifice and the need for redemption represented years later by the mystified atavism of novelist Yukio Mishima with his public *seppuku*, as it already had been represented by the suicide of Serizwa.

One could almost say, in retrospect, the beating Japanese cities have taken in *kaiju eiga* after *kaiju eiga*, even though by now reduced to kitsch-formulaic motifs repeated with no evident awareness of their roots in humiliation, mourning, and disorientation, represent a metaphorical form of ritual suicide, of atonement for defeat or, worse, the apostasy of surrender. As it was for James Joyce's Stephen Dedalus, history in *Gojira* is a nightmare from which Japan is unable to awaken. These epicyclic movie catastrophes are like acts of *seppuku*, simultaneously punishment and redemption, the nation commits with Gojira as its *tanto*. Whether these contexts were deliberate storytelling strategies of Honda, his co-scriptwriter Takeo Murata, or the original story

---

* For an excellent treatment of this issue, see Roy Andrew Miller's *Japan's Modern Myth* (Boston: Weatherhill, 1982).

VI. The Mythic and Religious Gojira

contributor Shigeru Kayama, is practically irrelevant. In the social and political world of mid-1950s Japan, they would play upon psychological and spiritual issues with which the film's audience would have been grappling and with which they would have been all too familiar.

Akira Ifukube, son of a Shinto priest and composer of *Godzilla*'s score, identified a key Japanese psychological and spiritual dichotomy in the 1998 BBC interview mentioned earlier: "The Japanese had fought with all their spirit but in the end it was technology that defeated them. Godzilla is undefeated by technology."* The problem is that, as a gigantic *hibakusha*, he is also an unintended *product* of it. Nevertheless, if as Ifukube infers Gojira is somehow a symbol of the Japanese spirit, what does his form and his behavior say about the state of that spirit at the time of the making of the film? Ifukube, no less than *Gojira*'s contemporary audiences, was surely aware that the popular term for the Japanese spirit, *yamatodamashii*, had, during the war years, become ideologically frontloaded through political manipulation. Nationalists used the phrase during the 1930s and throughout the Pacific War as a rallying cry, epitomizing the indomitability of the *Bushido* code. To whatever extent Gojira is a "warning" about the nuclear arms race, he is also a spiritual mirror Japan held up to itself, including, in Ifukube's sense, an incarnation of its own dark side, of the ideologically reconfigured medieval and Shogun-era beliefs that promulgated its delusions of invincibility and led it into a disastrous conflict. The *kaiju*, whatever else he may represent, is the revenant of *yamatodamashii* bearing the radioactive scars of its own unmaking.

Gojira first appears in the waters off Odo Island, a fictional location whose position on the sea charts at the Japan Coast Guard office places it within or very near the Izu archipelago, administrative outliers of Tokyo Prefecture. Several writers have placed Odo Island in the "south seas" or, in Noriega's case, "Micronesia" (69). Peter H. Brothers locates it in the Bonin Islands southwest of Japan. These locations are plainly wrong, as the coordinates given in the film by a security official for the frigates operating against Gojira off Odo Island's west coast are 136–138.07 E—33.04–33.08 N, within the general area of the Izu Archipelago, also called the Tokyo Islands. They lie at the outer edge of Sagami

---

* See the N.F. Jones' BBC documentary which includes interviews with members of the original *Gojira* crew and cast.

In Search of Godzilla

Bay, beginning about 60 km to the south of the entrance to Tokyo Bay. The Japanese mainland is distantly visible when the Eiko-Maru explodes, as well as during the depth-charge attack against Gojira by Japanese navy frigates.

When Yamane, Emiko, Ogata and Shinkichi watch a television report of the Japanese Coast Guard's depth charge attack on Godzilla, the announcer says the ships left port at 10 a.m. and began their attack off the west coast of Odo Island only 17 minutes later. Earlier, a Sikorsky H-19 helicopter, with a range of 400 miles and top speed of around 100 MPH, brought the first group of government officials and journalists to the island. The Japanese security forces were given several of these obsolescent aircraft during and right after the occupation. It wouldn't have had anything close to the range required to reach the Bonins, much less Micronesia, from Tokyo. It certainly wouldn't have been able to return to a distant Tokyo on the same tank of fuel even if Gojira's covering storm hadn't wrecked it. Moreover, the islanders have Japanese, not Micronesian, names like Shinkichi, Inada, and Izuma, the latter's name being something of a giveaway.

The location of Odo Island is interesting in a number of respects. For several years prior to the writing and filming of *Gojira*, the waters around and south of the Izu Archipelago already had a bad reputation in folklore and in the popular imagination. Like the Bermuda Triangle off the east coast of North America, the area was known for ship disappearances and was dubbed *ma no umi*, troublesome or dangerous waters, by the Japanese newspaper *Asahi Shimbun* as early as July 19, 1930. Representing Gojira as a local *kami* or folk legend, then, was an extension of the bad reputation the area already had.

The most relevant episode on that haunted sea, though, occurred on September 24, 1952, near the southeastern end of the archipelago. The 150-foot Japanese meteorological and geoscientific research vessel, the Kaiyō Maru Number Five was suddenly destroyed with the loss of all 31 crew and researchers as the Myōjin-shō underwater volcano it was studying suddenly erupted directly beneath it. The disaster, which carved out its own place in maritime lore, is specifically mentioned to Ogata and to the owner of the ill-fated *Eiko Maru* by a Japan Coast Guard official.

Virtually all critics of *Gojira* have pointed out how the fate of the *Eiko Maru* inflects the irradiation by fallout of the tuna boat Daigyo

VI. The Mythic and Religious Gojira

Fukuryu Maru, the Lucky Dragon Five, which sailed too close to the Castle Bravo hydrogen bomb test on Bikini atoll. However, what we see happen to the hapless *Eiko Maru* and subsequent ships incinerated from below is in fact much closer to what befell the Kaiyō Maru more than a year earlier. To demonstrate how the research vessel tragedy has lingered in the national memory, as the mysterious ship disasters pile up, "Undersea Volcano?" is one of the questions Japanese newspaper headlines rolling off the presses pointedly ask. This is just another example of how multi-layered, multi-referential so many of the metaphors woven through this movie really are. We will take a closer look at the volcanic tragedy, and its relevance to *Gojira*, in the "Godzilla Ecology" chapter below.

There is a vital tension whose focus is Odo Island between Gojira as protagonist of Odo Island folklore and his apparent origins in the depths of the far south central Pacific in the vicinity of the Marshall Islands. His return to the Izus transforms the sea lanes and especially Tokyo Bay into a myth haunted region. Like a true *kami* he is empowered to alter or deform the natural, to project his own deformities upon nature and civilization. He deforms time as well, revisiting the island with his very antiquity. The creature transits from its liminal habitat towards the numinous core of a reborn civilization by way of Odo, an interstitial zone haunted by its kami. The aged Izuma is the keeper and explicator of its secrets.

Odo Island is itself a legend-haunted area where prehistory and recent history blend into one another, and in the figure of our monster, ancient fears become indistinguishable from modern man's. That the village elder Izuma insists Gojira has always lived in the sea near Odo identifies the creature with traditional sea dragons of Japanese lore on one hand, but also suggests Gojira has traditionally navigated the sea bottom from his abyssal habitat far to the south where he was damaged by the H-bomb test to, perhaps, his feeding grounds near the island, where his presence adversely affects the fishing. We will also consider this likelihood in much greater detail in the "Godzilla Ecology" chapter below.

Meanwhile, Honda's geographical scenarios are important because the despoilage of uncorrupted economic and religious culture of Odo by modernity, and Gojira's destructive response to it, is allegorically central to the film's complex message. Supported by traditional dragnet fishing, the Izu Islands had no electricity until 1953. They embody the contrast between a still emerging modern postwar Japan and the fading away of more traditional cultural forms. The bent and broken telephone poles and electric lines on Odo mean the island has only recently joined modern Japan and in this sense we might read Gojira's depredations as another of the film's examples of ancient tradition striking back at its own abandonment. No sooner do they begin to modernize, in other words, than their local *kami* becomes *onryo*, or vengeful, and responds by savaging the community.

Jase Short has observed why in earlier science fiction films, especially the first generation of Japanese kaiju cinema, the legendary beasts of the ancients so often irrupt into modernity. "Most of the monsters in these early films are worshipped and revered by islanders and rural dwellers left behind by the vast changes of capitalist industrialization," Short points out. "Rather than representing hauntings of the new world by the old, kaiju came to be modernizations of old sensibilities run rampant. They grew to gargantuan sizes and enjoyed enormous destructive powers in order to concretize the sense that the old world had been thrown into a state of disarray" (68).

Gojira repeats his aversion to the modernized Japan in his first appearance in Tokyo Bay. Following the naval bombardment off the coast of Odo Island, Honda presents us with a panoramic view of the Ginza district. Bejeweled with neon signs and partygoers, the entertainment district pulses with optimism and relief. In the next scene a party boat, garishly lit up as though a fragment of the Ginza had broken off and sailed into the bay, runs afoul of Gojira. He suddenly emerges, only half a kilometer or so from the boat, and terrifies the reveling passengers. They rush from the party deck for the illusory safety of the cabins. Apparently satisfied he's stilled the noxious Hawaiian dance music emanating from the boat, he submerges again.

We understand by now how lucky the party boat passengers and crew have been. "In the movie, the inhabitants of Odo Island actually have a long standing belief in the existence of a creature they call 'Gojira' (Anglicized as Godzilla)," writes Stephanie Fay, and this creature "occasionally needs to be placated with a sacrifice when the fishing gets bad" (Deeper). The old fisherman Izuma explains Gojira as Odo Island's *ujigami*, a capricious patron deity. The elder's very name marks him as an autochthonous expression of the archipelago itself.

VI. *The Mythic and Religious Gojira*

Izuma's insistence Gojira has always been there and had been propitiated with sacrifices of young girls in the "old days"—which he discusses as though he can recall them—is one among many allusions linking the monster with the Shinto *kami Ryūjin*, greatest of the mythological sea dragons, as well as with the spiritual childhood of Japanese culture.

The *kami*'s name means "luminous being," which might well be parodied by the way Gojira's dorsal plates light up when he expectorates his radioactive aerosol. In his ancient knowledge Izuma also manifests Ryūjin's retainer, the lesser kami Ryuja, described in the 8th-century compendium *Kojiki* as having "the face of an old man." Izuma's weather-beaten face, mouth sharply downturned at its corners, suggests many ritual as well as *Noh* and *Kabuki* masks, a subject to which we will return in more detail below.

Another allusion to this mighty *kami* occurs as, fleeing down Hachiman Hill when Gojira suddenly rears up from behind it, Emiko falls and looks up to see the monster leaning over and roaring down at her. This scene appears based on Utagawa Kuniyoshi's famous nineteenth-century *ukiyo-e* woodblock print of Ryūjin menacing Princess Tamatori. Even in this memorable vignette Honda once again engages the problem of Japan's transition from living ancient lore to modernity. As the Princess Tamatori myth hearkens back to the age of ritual sacrifice, as described by Izuma, Emiko's invocation of the figure reminds us that ritual observation has evolved over the centuries from literal to symbolic re-enactment.

In Shinto myths Ryūjin is said to live in the deepest part of the ocean. Indeed, Dr. Yamane, in his lecture to the government committee upon his return from Odo Island after first sighting Gojira, points to the deepest part of the ocean on his geological chart to locate the "Jurassic strata" which is the monster's native habitat. Mark Anderson sites this aspect of the creature within the context of a wartime debate between Japanese scholars about the role of folklore in maintaining morale and defining Japanese culture against inroads of modernity. "[The Odo Island sequences suggest] the *Yanigata Kunio* school of folklore studies.... [which] argued that Okinawa and the Pacific islands were likely origins of Japanese culture and should be studied as such," Anderson notes. In this regard, Izuma's comments emphasize "the consequences of the loss that comes with neglecting traditional ways, and failing to respect and sustain indigenous, non–European–American identity" (27).*

The islanders perform a pacification or *kagura* ceremony to placate Gojira, which indicates they observe a form of *Ryūjin shinkō*, or sea dragon worship. Other observances of *Ryūjin shinkō* are commonly practiced by fishing communities to propitiate the *kami* and ensure good catches (Hiroshi). In an allusion to the fear of *genshi maguro*, or irradiated tuna, in the wake of the Lucky Dragon episode, which practically wrecked the Japanese fishing industry, the islanders perform their ritual not so much because they fear Gojira, but because their fishermen cannot catch anything. Finally, in this connection, after Gojira rears up over Hachiman Hill to terrify the crowd running up the path to an illusory safety, three islanders with samurai swords, including Inada-san, headman of the island, appear atop the hill after the creature disappears wraithlike back into the sea. They suggest an earlier era when myths of dragons migrated from China and took root in Japan.

Dragons are important *kami* throughout Shinto. However significant the influence of western monster movies like Willis O'Brien's *King Kong* were on the initial conceptualization and making of this film, Izuma represents Gojira not as a nuclear era mutant or prehistoric survival, but as a folkloric spirit bearing, in perverted form, many attributes of menacing sea monsters long resident in the national lore. Ryūjin is a lord of the oceans, patron of storms and floods, which he controls with his magical "Tide Jewels," a crèche of which he hides in his undersea lair. He is also patron spirit of fishing, good luck, and fertility, symbolic of the most basic energies of nature, of the *elan vital*.† Gojira is, in effect, a malignant *parody* of this *kami*, hideously deformed by nuclear blasts. Whereas throughout his many legends Ryūjin assures plentiful fishing, this unlucky dragon's appearance off Odo Island ruins the catch. In place of fertility, Gojira brings radioactive contamination. He is the entanglement, if not the unification, of the mythological and the pathological.

---

* And if all this weren't enough, the Hondas named their son Ryuji.

† For some general information on this, see, for example, M. Lindemans' entries on Ryujin at the *Encyclopedia Mythica* and at http://www.angelfire.com/falcon/ecsc-fwb/rj-md/DRAGON6.html.

VI. The Mythic and Religious Gojira

Like a spirit, Gojira's countenance is mercurial. His physiognomy changes from scene to scene, appearing more symmetrical, less radiation-scarred in distance shots but becoming more deformed in tighter frames. The face of the monster who first rises above Hachiman Hill on Odo Island is extensively scarred. It has a blunt snout, crooked jaws, and teeth which protrude crocodile-like from an only partially closable mouth. The Gojira who savages Tokyo, seen from a distance, has smoother features, with a more gently tapered snout and can close its mouth completely.

Even so, the more closely the monster can be seen, the more clearly perceived its deformities. Gojira's misshapen face in close-ups is a telltale sign of the hydrogen bomb tests which predicated his emergence from his abyssal habitat. However, those distortions also signify much more, given the monster's incarnation of traditional folkloric and mythic beings. In the nighttime sequences of its dual attacks on the city, the frontal view of Gojira's ravaged face with its glaring eyes resembles an *oni* mask, a Shinto messenger from hell or the tormented Buddhist afterlife. As a survivor of the Jurassic age and a dweller in abyssal regions, the creature is, after all, a messenger from the geological afterlife. Hell, or at least its closest simulacrum, had been visited on Japan in incendiary raids and nuclear attacks, and Gojira is plainly a revisitation of the latter.

Moreover, many types of *oni*, depicted in Noh dramas, Shinto ritual, and Buddhist iconography sport outsized glaring eyes, protruding fangs and jutting teeth. Gojira's resemblance to those masks in his closeup views, especially in a few frontal scenes, would have had a powerful impact on Japanese viewers who, since their childhood, have been exposed to rituals and performances which included those beings. Shinto spirits are notoriously mercurial, too, changing shape or posing as other beings. Thus, Gojira also belongs to a category of beings known as *bakemono* or shapeshifters: "During the Edo period, another word, bakemono, began appearing in all sorts of contexts, from illustrated books to Kabuki plays to misemono spectacle shows. Meaning literally 'changing thing' or 'thing that changes,' bakemono emphasizes transformation, a characteristic common to many yōkai" (Foster 17–18). Special effects master Eiji Tsuburaya utilized several different Gojira heads and torso mannequins. He surely was aware of the different configurations of each. Tsuburaya and Honda

In Search of Godzilla

leave us, quite deliberately, with the visual text of a shapeshifting spirit-monster.

Shinto themes are reinforced by several other images and allusions throughout the film. One is the exorcism ceremony Odo Islanders perform in an attempt to rid the surrounding waters of their ancient *kami* and restore their fishing. This *Kagura* dance performance, represented by Izuma as a *chinkon* or pacification ritual, consists of four dancing *yamabushi tengu*, spirits of warfare and of storms.* Protectors especially of the forests and mountains, the islanders invoke them to protect their waters from their threatening local demon. The *shimenawa*, ritual barrier cords meant to repel malign *kami* and *oni*, strung above the stage foreshadow the spectacular power line scene at the outset of the monster's second assault on Tokyo. Later that same night an unanticipated storm lashes Odo Island. Ryūjin is also a lord of tides and typhoons.† Rather than driving the troublesome *kami* from their waters, the *tengu* appear to have summoned it up with its accompanying tempest. Like Ryūjin, the monster unleashes his typhoon, enshrouded by which he makes his first appearance on land.

Another religious allusion occurs when Godzilla tears through a barrier of high-tension electrical lines which have been erected expressly to repel him and protect central Tokyo. The electrical lines also function as *shimenawa*, the same ritual cords put up around shrines, ceremonial sites, and even new construction as a barrier against *oni* and evil *kami*. Many *shimenawa* are traditionally decorated with *shide*, or zigzag lightning bolt designs; there are several of these lightning bolts hanging from the *shimenawa* above the shrine on Odo. When *shide* are attached to a wand, the resulting ritual implement, used in purification rituals, is known as a *haraegushi*, or lightning wand. Hence, the power lines and towers, which explode with electric arcs as Gojira lumbers through them, allegorize ritual implements meant to keep him from the numinous heart of the city.

On a grander scale than the Odo power poles, albeit in their same spirit, the postwar power grid in Japan, with its enormous towers crisscrossing the countryside, was symbolic of the nation's rebirth after

---

* See the *A to Z Dictionary of Japan's Buddhist Deities*.
† See the homepage of the *Encyclopedia of Shinto* in English.

VI. The Mythic and Religious Gojira

the devastation of the Pacific War.* Thus, in the film's most memorable battle set piece, Gojira's assault on the power lines also represents the triumph of the radiation-deformed *kami* over ritual ostracism for the second time. The first was his shrugging off of the Odo Island *yamabushi tengu*. In another instance of the ancient order lashing out at the new, Gojira exfoliates into his dragon *kami* identity precisely during this scene, unleashing his atomic aerosol against the high tension towers. Having violated the ritual barrier meant to protect a renascent Tokyo, the monster needs no further subterfuges and Japan's ancient spurned, damaged, and vengeful dragon god of the ancient order asserts itself unalloyed.

Ancient religious imagery isn't strictly allegorized by the form of the monster either. The breath is a critical symbol in Japanese Buddhism and Shinto. *Misogi-no-kokyu-ho*, purification through breathing, expresses the importance of respiration and represents the breath as an essence of spiritual life. This locates the oxygen destroyer within the extended symbolic system of Shinto, so that when Serizawa unleashes his weapon, he is also unleashing a curse, exterminating a spirit-being by attacking its very essence. It also reminds us, speaking of the monster's connection with Moby Dick, that the doomed Captain Ahab's final words are "I spit my last breath at thee!"

Gojira's atomic breath is an aerosol of caustic, irradiated venom. This interpretation of his "radioactive breath," like many other aspects of this classic film, is rooted in ancient Japanese dragon lore. According to Tsuda, aquatic dragons described in an ancient collection of Shinto folktales and myths, *Nihon Shoki* (ca. 720 AD), "emitted poisonous vapors and inflicted pains on the passers-by which often proved fatal" (761). Godzilla is, in other words, mythic in the sense he represents the very energy of nature with its benevolent functions perverted by atomic radiation or degraded into irremediable hostility. The first Japanese emperor, Jimmu,† was said to be the great-grandson of

---

* The power grid was also symbolic, in subtler ways, of some older traditions. Eastern and Western Japan actually have two separate power grids running on different transmission frequencies which were built by the American General Electric and the German AEG during the late 19th century. The grids must be reconciled at their meeting points by transformer centers. After World War II, rather than modernize the two grids into a single system, the Japanese merely rebuilt them on their old, disparate chasses.

† See http://www.ancientworlds.net/aw/Post/1261611. This website relates various ancient folktales.

In Search of Godzilla

Ryujin ("Ryujin"). The radioactive monster is thereby linked by legend to the imperial bloodline of the nation, indicative of how profoundly the atomic attacks have intoxicated its culture. *Gojira*, then, incubates a bitter post-imperial irony: nuclear testing forces the imperial ancestor to the surface, whereas the first time ordinary Japanese citizens heard the voice of the emperor was during his radio broadcast announcing the surrender of Japan, violating his ritual silence because of the dual atomic bombings.

In this connection, historian Yoshikuni Igarashi argues that the bomb and Hirohito were cast as analogues of each other in what he calls the "foundational narrative" of postwar Japanese-American political and cultural accommodation: both intervened in history to bring a halt to the war and peace to Japan (25–27). In effect, this narrative was meant to ameliorate the humiliation and sense of powerlessness, as well as Japanese fury and resentment of such a horrible weapon being used against them. At the same time, it also re-legitimized the emperor's continuing reign, even if as just a figurehead, by emphasizing his visionary role as peacemaker. If we consider for a moment Gojira's identification with the deity Ryujin as well as with the atomic bomb, Igarashi's carefully balanced political analogy becomes a freighted, and unstable, mythopoeic constellation of clashing affects. In his words, given this symbolic amalgam at the time of his appearance on the cultural scene, Godzilla—as Igarashi refers to him—would necessarily appear "monstrous":

> Memories of the war, even without specific markers, were still ubiquitous in postwar society. However, increasingly removed from the scene of destruction and devoid of particular references, the memories were transformed into amorphous destructive forces. Monstrous forms that defy human comprehension were burdened with the mission to represent memories of war loss. The film *Gojira* (Godzilla) is one such product of the specific historical conditions of mid–1950s Japan, from which markers of loss were steadily disappearing [114].

Igarashi argues that "the narrative of Godzilla operates within the discursive space of the foundational narrative" insofar as it "effaces" markers of loss and relegates them to "the abject," which he defines as "that which is constitutive of history but cannot be named" (215). I would argue the opposite. For a Japan trying to move beyond the Pacific War, Gojira brings history to a standstill. In his identification

VI. The Mythic and Religious Gojira

with Ryujin, Gojira *destabilizes* the foundational narrative, such as it is, and is far too vividly an objectification of the atomic bomb to deflect the naming of his origin. Furthermore, in his re-staging of the Ryujin mythos the monster returns its audience, in more than the merely subconscious sense, to an antecedent cultural ethos which had been a prime target of Occupation repression.

Old Izuma, who explains the legend of Gojira as well as the islanders' ceremony of expiation to Hagiwara (and angrily justifies it to some of Odo's skeptical young women), behaves like Ryujin's mythical messenger, Riuja, whom the *Nihon Shoki* describes as having "the face of an ancient man." Izuma's claim that he remembers when young girls were sacrificed to Godzilla is remarkable since human sacrifices had ceased in Japan in very ancient times. We can interpret this as the confusion on the part of an elderly man of recollection of folk tales with actual recollection of events, or as evidencing how strongly Izuma identifies with the ancient traditions. However, his memory identifies him, at least allegorically, as belonging to the realm of the Ryujin myths in the role of the kami's messenger.

Furthermore Izuma's wonderfully expressive face, as portrayed by veteran actor Kokuten Kôdô, is characterized by his starkly downturned mouth, a grimace revealing his disdain for modernity and resentment of being treated like a relic by the younger Odo women. From another point of view Izuma's wise, sad face invokes many of the physiognomic qualities of Professor Yamane, the only other character who is aware of Gojira as an ancient sea creature originating during the Cretaceous period. One could say that while Yamane gives us the scientific explanation for Gojira's roots and reappearance, Izuma supplies us with his mythic, folkloric and ritual aspect.

Ancient tales of sacrifices to Ryujin were commonplace. According to Naratake Tsuda, the *Nihon Shoki* contains several such narratives:

When Prince Yamatodake was crossing the sea to subjugate a revolt in the east, his boat was nearly capsized by a sudden storm. But his consort, Tachibana-hime, thinking it to be a punishment visited upon them by the deity of the sea, threw herself into the deep to calm the agitation of the waves, and thus the life of the prince was saved. There is a slightly different story in the *Tailieiki*, written in the fourteenth century. A passenger boat was passing through Xaruto of Awa when it suddenly stopped in a whirlpool and could not proceed. The passengers conjectured this was

In Search of Godzilla

caused by Riujin, the dragon deity, with the intention of getting something in their possession. They threw their swords and armor, and other things which they thought the deity coveted, into the water. But the whirlpool would not become calmer. Meanwhile a steersman crying out from below said that the place being the eastern gate of Riu-gu ("Dragon Palace"), some precious thing should be given the dragon for regaining their freedom [763].

Izuma/Riuja, then, constructs Gojira, sacrifices and all, as a symbol of the lost innocence of his race. After warning his fellow islanders that they must have angered Gojira, the fishwives standing behind him dismiss his concerns by laughing "Old Izuma and Gojira—both relics of the past."* Their exchange alerts us once again to how deeply this film operates in the realm not merely of recent history but of myth. It behaves as though history, prehistory and mythic time were folded over each other like the ancient geological strata from Professor Yamane's charts. Izuma's "recollection" of maiden sacrifices also anticipates, if not predicates, the scene wherein Gojira leans over the crest of Hachiman Hill above Odo Island's sole village and roars down at the terrified Emiko Yamane, who has tripped over a root and fallen. Ogata races back to her, lifts her in his arms, and hides with her in the underbrush.

This scene is reminiscent of Jack Driscoll's rescue of perpetual blonde Ann Darrow from King Kong, in the eponymous film which influenced so many aspects of the original Toho production of *Gojira*. Ogata is a marine officer which further parallels Ann Darrow's romance with first mate Driscoll, whom she meets on the ship en route to Skull Island. The question of how or when Emiko and Ogata originally met might be answered, "in *King Kong*."

Within moments of this horrifying episode Gojira has disappeared back into the sea. There is no mistaking such an allegorical, if displaced, re-enactment of Izuma's ancient sacrificial ritual. Of the common motifs of myths wherein maidens are sacrificed to dragons, many were also collected in the *Kojiki*, a compendium of myths and folklore from early in the eighth century AD. About these stories Tsuda writes: "There are three elements in these tales of a serpent being killed, viz., the monster wants human sacrifices, a girl to be sacrificed is rescued, and the

---

* See *Encyclopedia Mythica*, a website dedicated to Japanese folk deities.

VI. The Mythic and Religious Gojira

rescued girl is married to the hero by whom she is saved. These elements reappear very often in the later folktales of a similar nature" [762].

Tsuda recounts in addition to human sacrifices to aquatic dragons, the other common tale of human sacrifice in Japanese myth and lore involves malignant giant monkey deities (764–65). This is noteworthy because the monster's Japanese name, Gojira, is in partial deference to King Kong a contraction of the words for "gorilla" and "whale."

Aside from her Tamatori correspondence, Emiko displays other mythic affinities when she intercedes with Dr. Serizawa to use the oxygen destroyer against Gojira. Her actions identify her with the benevolent Buddhist deity of the sea, Benten.* In various myths and legends, Benten is both the bride of a dragon and, as a folk derivation of the Buddhist *Taras*, or tears, of compassion who defends mankind against evil dragons. Emiko breaks down and weeps on several occasions, which I suppose is preferable to her predecessor Ann Darrow's constant screaming in *King Kong*.

Benten is also depicted as a patron deity of music, and at the beginning of *Gojira* Emiko is dispatched by Ogata, who must report to work due to the sinking of the Eiko-Maru, to a Budapest String Quartet concert they had planned to attend. Ogata is a professional salvage diver, which further links him to the sea spirits with whom Benten, as well as Ryujin, often consort (Broomcloset, "Benten").

Gojira/Ryujin's appearance in his irradiated, or westernized, form is a revisitation of spiritual childhood, of mother earth, to the Odo islanders. When a security official complains to Dr. Yamane the government will have to close all shipping lanes if they can't find a solution to the Godzilla "problem," he ironically invokes the seventeenth-century Tokugawa imposition of *sakoku*, or isolationism. This policy was meant to interdict Christian, i.e., western, inroads against the nation's Buddhist and animist religious culture. *Sakoku* insulated Japan from European and American influence for nearly 250 years until Commodore Perry forced open the doors in 1853. As a bit of delicious irony, Japan was commemorating the centennial of Perry's incursion, for better or worse, at about the same time as *Gojira* began to take shape at Toho Studios.

---

*See the blog entry at "The Broomcloset," http://broomcloset.wordpress.com/2013/03/08/benten-japanese-goddess-of-eloquence/.

In Search of Godzilla

The unmistakable parallelism between Odo and *sakoku* Japan is a microcosm of Japanese religious history. Yamane's research party, disembarked from their vessel, wanders up a lane through the demolished village between tilted telephone poles, stripped of their wires like desecrated crucifixes. These suggest the Christian genocide of the *sakoku* period as vividly depicted in Shusaku Endo's troubling novel *Silence*, wherein suspected Japanese Christians were forced to desecrate Christian icons, including stepping on them, to prove their Shinto or Buddhist loyalties. The downed telephone or electric wires on the island, once again, suggest violated *shimenawa*. The little island, like the Japan of those years, is similarly isolated by sea. When the government research vessel bearing Dr. Yamane and his fellow scientists and their Geiger counters breaks the monster's *de facto* sea blockade, contact with modernity is restored. It is precisely with the arrival of these scientists that the monster finally shows himself in daylight, towering above the hills behind the island's village roaring angrily, as if to protect his reestablished mythic ethos.

Even in their waning belief in their titular kami the islanders nonetheless observe ancient rituals of dragon worship known as *Ryūjin shinkō*. According to Iwai Hiroshi in *The Encyclopedia of Shinto*, these rituals have to do with propitiation of the water deity to bring rain. Unfortunately, the ceremony the islanders perform as an exorcism inadvertently brings the storm veiled by which Gojira first emerges. It is almost as if so much time has passed since the last time the natives had to resort to this ceremony, they have lost touch with its meteorological function and misapplied it with disastrous results.

When secular, mainland Japanese first arrive in their helicopter, unannounced (as Gojira will soon arrive as well), they seem to sense the strangeness of the place. The visitors look partially baffled; note the expression on the journalist Hagiwara's face when he emerges from the helicopter. But then Odo is also a transitional space, like a stopping off point for the monster on his journey towards the Japanese heartland. The young women mocking Izuma's belief in Gojira, thereby disconnecting themselves from the island's history, is another of the film's numerous examples of traditions in decay. It mirrors the main example of that decay, namely, Emiko's defiance of her betrothal to Serizawa. The contrast between the islanders' dismissal of Izuma's conviction Gojira has returned to plague them and subsequent staging of an ancient

VI. The Mythic and Religious Gojira

ceremony to exorcise the ancient Shinto demigod exemplify the mid-century Japanese soul divided against itself.

The famous commuter train vignette in the unbowdlerized film, which was deliberately exorcized from the Transworld version, is yet another example of this. A pair of Tokyo salarymen and a secretary discuss the sea monster and link it to the "contaminated tuna" from the Lucky Dragon 5, and to evacuation shelters during the terminal stages of the Pacific War. This scene demonstrates how vividly contemporaneous Japanese, especially urban dwellers, remembered the war and its horrifying conclusion. Their western dress and their "commuter" working status demonstrate as powerfully as their mordant expressions of frustration how much they would like to move on from wartime Japan, with its anachronistic valorization of Bushido codes, to embrace the Spenglerian "civilized" phase of modern Japan. The radiation-deformed *kami* thus suspends history for them, as well as for the Odo islanders. *Gojira* is, in this sense, a catalogue of the spiritual and psychological price the islanders, like the Tokyo commuters, would have to pay to join the modern world.

The rustic world of Odo Island contrasts sharply with a Tokyo rebuilt in western mode, although the island is administratively infiltrated by civilized authority and dotted with telephone poles, many leaning woefully (suggesting the exterminated Christians of the *sakoku* period) after the island has been battered by the storm-shrouded Gojira. Moreover, Yamane's "research expedition" to Odo features a Geiger counter examination of a contaminated well and one of Gojira's footprints. The tests lead to the discovery of a trilobite—another symbol of Oswald Spengler's "spiritual childhood" and "Mother Earth." Admonished about holding it in his hand by Professor Tanabe, a radiologist, because the trilobite is radioactive, Yamane puts it in a box and immediately begins prowling the footprint for more of them.

Mother Earth is here directly contrasted with the modern instrument and its apocalyptic symbolism. We see the same Professor Tanabe taking a Geiger counter reading on a refugee child after Godzilla's march through Tokyo, then shaking his head sadly, which must have jarred an audience barely nine years removed from Hiroshima and Nagasaki. Near the film's climax, Tanabe holds the sensor near the water's surface from the deck of the warship carrying the oxygen destroyer. The Geiger counter in search of Godzilla follows him throughout the narrative like Jacques Derrida's phallic indicator.

In Search of Godzilla

Given how both its director and the composer of its soundtrack were the sons of clergymen, it should be no surprise that deep skeins of religious symbolism run throughout *Gojira*. In what seems to me a wonderful irony, Honda, the son of a Buddhist priest, a faith that acknowledges an essential void, approached Ifukube early in the summer of 1954 as the production of *Gojira* was getting underway and asked him to imbue his monster with spirit. "I know very little about music, but I know I have created a fake monster," he told Ifukube, whose father was a Shinto priest. "Your music must breathe life into it" (Jones).

Before concluding this discussion, I don't want to overlook how Christian history, hagiography, and theology are also deployed in *Gojira*. When Yamane is being questioned by a government official apparently connected to the security services about how Gojira can be killed, he responds, "Gojira was *baptized* [italics mine] in the fire of the hydrogen bomb and survived." The inferences of this phrase are several. It has its religious implications relating to childbirth, as if to say the beast had been birthed into the world by nuclear fire instead of holy water, a bitter enough irony in itself. Beyond that, the relationship of nuclear radiation to childbirth was becoming nightmarishly apparent in Japan as the film was being made and released, as the children of *hibakusha* in particular but of others related to them by marriage or proximity began to be stillborn, born with deformities, or develop early childhood cancers at an unprecedented rate. Serizawa's solicitude for his only working oxygen destroyer also manifests this childbirth imagery at the conclusion of the story as Yamane and Emiko hand it to him, cradled like a newborn, and he fondles and caresses it as would a new father his infant offspring. It is a bizarre if poignant spectacle.

Both Nagasaki and Hiroshima, the two atomic bomb targets, had sizable Christian populations. Nagasaki, in fact, had the largest Christian population in Japan. I mentioned above the persecution of Japanese Christians during the *Sakoku* period, the end of which ushered in that problematic era of rapid westernization so pertinent to *Gojira*'s themes of cultural criticism. Following the Meiji restoration's proclamation of religious liberalism in 1871 the Christian population of Japan grew to around 110,000. Nearly half of them lived in Nagasaki, and most of those were killed in the atomic bombing (Okuyama 64). So, there is a bitter irony in the notion that Christian America annihilated nearly

VI. The Mythic and Religious Gojira

half the Christian population of the mostly Buddhist and animist country in a single stroke. Nagasaki may have been the largest population, but Hiroshima had 13 Christian churches and an apostolic vicarage at the time of its bombing three days earlier. August 6, the date of the Hiroshima catastrophe, is also the date of the fiery Transfiguration of Christ in the Catholic Church calendar, adding another layer of irony to Yamane's observation that Gojira had been "baptized" by hydrogen bomb testing.

Having also discussed the disposition of Odo Island in terms of *sakoku* Japan, I should mention again the broken and twisted cruciform telephone and electric poles foregrounded in the scenes of the island's trampled village. We see them again as Honda's camera pans the devastated Tokyo of Gojira's passage beginning at 1:09:15, which fades into scenes of emergency units wearing red cross armbands carrying the injured into hospitals. All of this is to emphasize the reach of Honda's vision. The clergyman's son has been, if you will, quite catholic in his amalgamation of mythic, religious, and historical symbolism into its complex fabric.

VII

Visual Poetics

Gojira *as Ritual and Noh Performance*

As we have hinted several times above, *Gojira* is indebted for much of its underlying aesthetic power to Japanese theatrical traditions and ritual forms. Whereas it is true that Eiji Tsuburaya wanted to use cutting edge stop motion animation to bring his monster to life, once it became apparent budgetary and production scheduling constraints made that impossible, he and his crew defaulted to a more traditional esthetic. "What is poorly understood," writs J.I. Carrozza, "is that the art form of tokusatsu is intended to have an unreal, theatrical pantomime beauty" (13). The theater in Japan is itself deeply rooted in religious practice and drew its mythical and monstrous characters from rites and folk tales.

In *Japanese Plays*, A.L. Sadler observes that "the theatrical conventions of Noh, especially, evolved out of Shinto rituals and even the form and structure of the Shinto shrine" (Kindle ed. 186) Furthermore, although "Shinto is the dominant provider of stories and sources.... Buddhism flavors the plays, and the narrator-figure (*waki*) is likely to be a Buddhist monk. Thus the introducing character or Deuteragonist is as often as not a Buddhist monk with his characteristic phrase, '*Shōkoku Ikken no sō nite sōrō*—I am a priest traveling round the sights of my country'" (Kindle ed. 193–198).

The father of Ishiro Honda was himself a Buddhist priest, who moved his family from place to place as he was attached to various shrines, whereas Akira Ifukube, who composed the score for *Gojira*, was the son of a Shinto shrine keeper. According to Sadler, Noh stories were derived from myths and legends associated with particular shrines and temples, and important festivals usually featured a Noh play cycle held at the shines themselves (loc 175–177). Thus, many of the stories

VII. Visual Poetics: Gojira *as Ritual and Noh Performance*

about mythic or folk monsters are extremely localized. Both the young Ishiro Honda and Akira Ifukube would doubtless have been exposed to them and aware of their persistent indigeneity. Gojira's special affiliation with Odo Island would be more the rule than the exception to how Shinto promulgates its *kami*.

Perhaps, then, it is not coincidental or even ironic that Gojira's first venture ashore on Odo Island is preceded that same night by a *kagura* ceremony staged at the island's Shinto shrine.* Ifukube wrote the music for that ceremony. "Japanese monster movies did not emerge from a void in 1954," argue Rhoads and McCorkle, "nor did they merely copy or imitate Hollywood monster-on-the-loose films like *King Kong*. Instead, *kaiju eiga* and their aesthetics draw from a font of inspiration anchored in Japanese theater, mythology, and religious traditions with deep roots in Japanese society and culture" (31–32).

The solemn, resonating footfalls which precede Gojira's appearances recall the beat of the large *ōdaiko* drums used in both ritual and theatrical forms closely derived from it, a tradition of percussion with shamanic roots. Ifukube said he accidentally discovered the appropriate sound for the monster's footfalls when he knocked over an amplifier and was surprised by the resonant *booommm* it produced. The resemblance of that sound to the ritual and theatrical drum was serendipitous, because it enhances both the ancient ritual and more recent Noh sensibility of the film. Those thundering footsteps are symbolic more than literal portents since we hear them before we see the creature, even before he emerges from underwater. Once he is abroad and in plain sight, we do not hear them anymore. The sound of the monster's footfalls becomes a summons to ritual, opening a deformed version of the sacred space the drumbeats define upon the temple portico or the stage.

The first time we hear those deafening sounds is during the opening credits of the film, repeated thrice on the fourth beat followed by the first of several roars, then alternating with those roars but still on the fourth beat. During the *kagura* ritual the islanders conduct to mollify their aggravated *kami*, the *taiko* drum follows the same four beat pattern. We don't see the *hiyashi*, or musical ensemble, who perform the

---

* For more on *Kagura* dance and its roots in ancient pre-noh Shinto ritual, see David Petersen, *Invitation to Kagura: Hidden Gem of the Traditional Japanese Performing Arts* (Morrisville: Lulu Press, 2007).

gagaku ritual music, but in addition to the sound of the bamboo flute or *fue*, we can hear the *keisu* bowl gong, a smaller staccato drum which is probably a *tentekomai* or *denden*, and the larger, portentous taiko drum. "Taiko are used in Noh and Kabuki plays, to create moods and settings and to mimic animal sounds, wind, the sea, and thunder," notes the *New World Encyclopedia* (online).

In *Gojira*, the transition from the ritual music to the sounds of the storm and the first appearance abroad of Gojira himself is seamless. The flute gives way to the howl of wind, the percussion to crashing waves, thunder followed by the monster's booming footsteps, still distant, again on the fourth beat, growing louder as the creature approaches. In short order we hear Gojira's first roar whereupon Masaji looks through his window as a flash of lightning reveals the looming monster just outside. The entire sequence, from the ritual through Gojira's nocturnal advent, is perfectly executed with the music, especially the percussion, blending into the sounds of the storm and the beast.

Of the five main Noh types, three are relevant to our discussion: the *kami* or god play, which is the story of a shinto shrine; the *kichiko* or demon play, which features devils, strange beasts, and supernatural beings, and the *gendai mono* or contemporary play. The first relates to the Odo Island shrine which, we might offer, is the spiritual home or residence of the *kami* Gojira. Only when his ceremony is performed does the creature finally emerge from the sea as though to reclaim his turf. *Gojira* as a demon play is fulfilled by the monster's malevolent and destructive aspect. We have mentioned above his *oni*-like appearance and shapeshifting qualities, so similar to classic demon masks in both Shinto ritual and the Noh dramas which derived from them. In its simultaneous function as *gendai mono*, *Gojira* evokes the recent cataclysm of the Pacific War, the suppression and decline of so many elements of traditional cultural practices, and certainly not least it evokes the ravages of nuclear weaponry and testing.

In addition, many of these play forms featured a young boy, or *kokata*. The *kokata*'s function can be complex, sometimes intended to de-emphasize the importance of secondary figures around the *shite* or primary character. More often though, the *kokata* is portrayed as a traveling companion or *waki*, and often subordinate to the narrator or *kyogen*. Shinkichi, the orphaned teenager from Odo Island who is absorbed into the Yamane household, fulfills the function of the *kokata* in Gojira.

VII. Visual Poetics: Gojira *as Ritual and Noh Performance*

If one were to catalogue objections to any aspect of *Gojira*, dissatisfaction with flaws in its special effects, the shortcomings of Eiji Tsuburaya's "Suitmation" approach to representing the monster, would doubtless head the list. Critics either spend their time attacking its lack of "realism," or compositing apologia for it. Such criticism became inevitable once Tsuburaya and his cohorts decided O'Brien-Harryhausen style stop motion animation would be too time consuming and expensive. The film, whose production began in the spring of 1954, had to be completed by November of that year. It was trapped by the evacuated production schedule of the cancelled Tomoyuki Tanaka vehicle *In the Shadow of Glory*. If production were to run overtime it would also become too costly for Toho's budget, already being stretched by the production of Kurosawa's *Seven Samurai*.

On the other hand those who praise the production values of *Gojira* point out how well the filmmakers managed to create their effects, given Toho's budgetary limitations or the technology available to them, primitive by comparison with the stop motion animation of American monster and fantasy films, much less contemporary CGI techniques. This perpetual argument, especially particular to Japan's genre of *kaiju* films, evokes the problem of "willing suspension of disbelief" versus the film's indebtedness to traditional Japanese theatrical aesthetics. "We want our money's worth in the form of a quick visceral fix of realistic sound and visual effect. We seem to be increasingly short on imagination and want not to be bothered suspending our disbelief," wrote Galbraith about the impatience of modern audiences in *Monsters Are Attacking Tokyo* (11). Both sides of the argument, staged in this manner, assume that "realism" is always the goal of *tokusatsu* special effects. No, it isn't.

In Japanese theater and in its tokusatsu film alike, aesthetic seduction is the goal. In the case of *Gojira* that seduction depended upon appealing to the dramatic forms most familiar to its domestic audience. Ironically enough, the same constraints of budget and schedule which forced Tsuburaya's recourse to that bulky suit also left him with a visual text in which Noh– and Kabuki–like movements became *de rigueur* for his monster, and opened an opportunity to introduce an aesthetic familiar to his audience in an unfamiliar new genre. The limited movements of the creature suit could be framed not only as suggestive of atomic flash burned hibakusha but, simultaneously, as *kata*, the stylized, compressed formal motions of the Noh performer. It was a fortuitous conjunction:

> The most basic kata from which all other movement is based is called *kame*. This is the basic posture for the Noh performer. In the lower body the knees are slightly bent, lowering the center of gravity of the performer. In the upper body the arms are slightly bent, elbows out, making a kind of circle shape with the arms....*

This closely described Gojira's posture during his usual locomotion. Observe him walking through the Shinagawa rail yards during his first excursion ashore in Tokyo, for example. Then watch him execute a shift in direction called *hakobi* at approximately 58:20, or just as the two fire trucks flip over while trying to avoid smacking into him.

Concerning Haruo Nakajima's performance as Gojira, according to the seminal text of Noh, the early fifteenth-century *Fushikaden* of Zeami Motokiyo, the essence of Noh is *monomanae* or imitation. In turn, Zeami's philosophy stresses the principle of *yugen*, the revelation of hidden beauty, of that which in the banal world is endarkened, beneath the surface. Actors are encouraged to perform using spare or symbolic movements. Noh does not aim at "realistic depiction, but rather at the very essence of the person, demon or god being portrayed" (cited in Wilson 5). Nakajima sought advice from Eiji Tsuburaya about how to move in the bulky monster suit, and the *tokusatsu* master advised him to avoid the appearance of human locomotion (Brothers 63).

The limitations on movement eventuated by the cumbersome suit abetted the actor's efforts to be monster-like instead of human-like, but there was more to it than that. Spending time at the Tokyo Zoo, Nakajima observed the movements of large animals like bears and lions, seeking to incorporate the essence of their locomotion into his performance, creating a locomotive impression distinctly Gojira's. As Zeami further declared, "No matter what kind of character you are playing, you must first learn to become the thing itself" (cited in Wilson 5). Nakajima was intensely faithful to Zeami's dictum. Zeami also cited the distinction between essence and function—"What is seen with the mind is essence, and what is seen with the eyes is function," he wrote (Zeami, *Shikado* cited in Wilson 6).

---

*https://www.the-noh.com/en/world/danceform.html.

VII. Visual Poetics: Gojira *as Ritual and Noh Performance*

Furthermore, Gojira's landward ponderousness—unsurprising for a creature accommodated to deep sea life—further serves to maintain the aesthetic continuity of his presentation. An unanticipated consequence of Nakajima's difficulties with the suit is that the monster's belabored progress on land, especially his stumbles at (51:42), further suggest a massive aquatic creature coping with its lost buoyancy. On the other hand, "The awkward movements of the monster enhance the irrational nature of its destructive acts," notes Igarashi. "The technology that produced Godzilla improved over the years, but this improvement adversely affected the artistic effects of the production" (118). Indeed. Those very limitations of budget and cinematic technology, the black and white cinematography with its dependence on shadow and light for effect, all contribute to the film's complexity and folkloric rusticity.

Suitmation technique, though, is not the only effects approach comparable to Noh stagecraft. Puppet theater appeared in Japan as early as the eleventh century. In the early nineteenth century it evolved into its most sophisticated form, *Bunraku*, with elaborate scripts and musical accompaniments:

> Bunraku is a deeply embedded portion of Japanese culture and history and may explain why early kaiju, the "man in a rubber suit" films, relied on puppetry and miniatures, even though other techniques existed.... In spite of this, and the relative box office success of these stop-motion films, Toho continued to rely primarily on a form of physical storytelling that closely mimics the style of bunraku [Barr 29].

Tsuburaya utilized a Gojira puppet built from the torso up in several scenes, including the monster's first appearance above Hachiman Hill on Odo Island. Closeups of its head and shoulders as it expectorates its radioactive breath, and the scene in which Gojira bites through a broadcast tower and sends a group of journalists plunging to their deaths all utilized the puppet.

Thus the monster stages multiple allusions to Japanese ritual and theatrical forms as well as recent history. Its posture and gestures, or brevity of same, betoken more than the stiffness and partial paralysis of the *hibakusha* even though the creature cannot help invoking their plight. It also walks slowly and stiffly in the manner of a Noh or Kabuki performer. Gojira's deportment ameliorates the artificiality of the "Godzilla suit" effect by encouraging viewers to "read" spectacle through a theatrical aesthetic. This phenomenon was a key to the film's record-busting financial success as well as its lasting appeal. Watching Noh performers clad in their spirit masks and elaborate costumes, Japanese audiences, like the worshipers of performers at religious shrines, are drawn by faith and awe into the spirit-realm not so much of the actors but of the deities and *kami* they behold. Our beleaguered but indomitable Haruo Nakajima, in his overheated costume, consummates millennia of composited Shinto and, eventually, Noh performance.

Gojira's countenance with its baleful eyes, exaggerated frontal fangs, and usually gaping mouth is clearly meant to composite the saurian with the supernatural. Just as old Izuma's face conjures up the expressions of dramatic and ritual masks, Gojira's physiognomy suggests the grotesque features of *oni* and spirit masks used in Noh plays. According to Tian Min, "The oni masks used in Noh drama were designed to emphasize their ugly and fearsome features." Writing about the demon roles in Noh drama, a performance specialty of the Yamato School, Zeami maintained that "[t]he essence of such roles lies in forcefulness and frightfulness." Thus the appearance of Gojira is rooted in a tradition of fearsome disguise which evolved over a millennium of ritual performances, dating as far back, and originating as far away, as China and Korea, out of which the drama developed. Min elaborates:

> The Nuo mask and the tsuina mask share the same function in Chinese and Japanese rites of exorcism. In both cases the mask externalizes and personifies human beings' desire and fear of the Other, either godly or ghostly, in their pursuit of communal prosperity, spiritual renewal, and auspicious protection from adverse natural and supernatural forces. The act of putting on the mask completes the dissolution of the Self and its identification with the godly or ghostly Other. The mask with all its manifestation of sacred and magic power was treated with utter reverence from its creation to its sanctification in a ritual enactment. In the Nuo and Tsuina rites and in early Noh and Nuoxi history, the making of the mask was, first of all, a sacred religious act of devotion rather than an artistic creation for the sake of aesthetic beauty and appreciation, as would be the case with later practices of Noh and Nuoxi in their more secular and refined forms [Min, *Chinese*].

From another perspective, Gojira's rampage levels the clutter of Tokyo to the bare essentials of the Noh stage. One of the conventions of that stage was a background representation of the Yōgō Pine, the axial tree at the Kasuga Shrine in Nara where, Shinto legend tells us, the gods

VII. Visual Poetics: Gojira *as Ritual and Noh Performance*

first descended to Earth. In *Gojira* that pine is effectively replaced by the mushroom cloud of the nuclear explosion which, as Ogata argues to Professor Yamane, "still haunts us Japanese." As the mushroom cloud stands in for the Yōgō pine, Gojira is its *kodama*, or resident spirit. Kodama also means echo, and Gojira is certainly an echo of catastrophes past.

On the other hand, we don't want to push the comparisons with Noh too far. The influence of traditional theatrical forms on Gojira, while extensive, are also subtle and rooted as much in a shared cultural milieu as in any overt intent on the part of the film's creators to directly transfer elements of Noh to the screen. "Noh theater, with its strict emphasis on structure and character roles, is often too confining to make the leap to film in its entirety," writes Barr. Nonetheless "the first [Gojira] film, with its heavy embrace of structure, silence versus music, and strict characterization, matches up nicely with Noh storytelling tradition" (34). Barr also claims that *Gojira* ends in silence, which would be very Noh-like—except that it really doesn't, from the haunting Ifukube score, to Ogata screaming into his microphone to the suicidal Serizawa, to the oxygen destroyer bubbling away, to Serizawa's "Live happily with Emiko," to Gojira's dying roar, to Yamane's grim prediction of another Gojira. The film ends on a forlorn note indeed, but hardly on a silent one.

VIII

Godzilla Ecology

> Why such a creature would appear in our territorial waters is the next question.
> —Professor Yamane

WE HAVE THUS FAR CONSIDERED *Gojira* from historical, sociopolitical, mythological, religious, and theatrical perspectives. Based on what we know from the film itself, particularly from a combination of Odo Island legend and Dr. Yamane's speculation, we can also construct a profile of how Godzilla conducted his natural affairs both before and after his exposure to the hydrogen bomb tests set him in motion against the extra-marine world. In an early production meeting among the film's top crew, Ishiro Honda said, "let us think of [Gojira] as real, not just a ridiculous monster created by bombs." Those who did not feel they could take the story seriously were politely disinvited from the project (Brown 28).

Yes, let us think of him that way. Much of how Godzilla functions as an organism—feeding, migrating, even responding to external stimuli—is left unstated in Honda and Murata's screenplay, but they do leave us with clues. In this section I propose a natural history—what in Japanese scholarship of the paranormal was designated *yōkaigaku*, or "monsterology" (Foster, *The Book of Yōkai* 52)—of Gojira. This approach will not resolve the film's essential tension between Gojira represented as an organism among other organisms and Gojira as a spirit, legend, or Shinto deity. Nor is it meant to. He is all those things at once, and to better comprehend him our thinking needs to encompass the ironies of his multiple, often contradictory, roles.

In his exposition before the diet committee following their Odo Island encounter, Yamane speculates that Gojira represents a lineage which has remained hidden for eons only to re-emerge due to nuclear

VIII. Godzilla Ecology

testing. In ecocritical terms Gojira, like the living trilobite the professor finds in the monster's footprint on Odo Island, is what paleontologists and biologists call a Lazarus taxon, a species which has gone missing from the fossil record but, like the coelacanth, is subsequently found alive. As the monster who stalks us through our nightmares he has his own, quite profound, connection to the film's concerns with environmental damage. This connection is largely unstated until Dr. Yamane's melancholy comment at the conclusion of the film that continued nuclear testing is liable to roust another of his species into collision with civilization. Writes Hillman:

> [Monsters] live in the repressed which returns, in the psychopathologies of instinct which assert themselves ... primarily in the nightmare and panic qualities. Thus the nightmare indeed gives the clue to the re-approximation to lost, dead nature. In the nightmare, repressed nature returns, so close, so real that we cannot but react to it naturally ... screaming out, asking for light, comfort, contact [32].

Destroy any more of this animal's habitat and another one, if not more, will in due time be upon us.

Yet Kyohei Yamane, dogged empiricist, is open to this conundrum precisely because it galvanizes his scientific curiosity. As he professes to the diet committee while suggesting a research party be organized to study Odo Island, there are mysteries in the Himalayas as well as mysteries "we cannot imagine" in the unexplored abysses of the sea. Joyce E. Boss has observed, "The Godzilla of the Odo Island legend is a terrifying and unpredictable force who wreaks havoc in his wake, and whose powers indicate the living dynamic forces at work in this world just beyond mundane everyday reality" (105). He is an embodiment both of the mysteries of nature and of myth at once, and this oxymoronic quality is a crux of his enduring fascination. And for Jason Barr, "The Odo Island villagers represent the old, loosely organized feudal Japan, in which belief systems varied widely and depended on natural observations: if there are no fish in the nets, something must be eating them" (78).

We can, however, debunk some common misreadings of what sort of organism Gojira is, where he came from and what forced him to the surface, all based on clues and inferences supplied by the film itself. Such an approach fits nicely with both Ishiro Honda and Shigeru Kayama's own fascination with nature. "I've always been interested in the natural sciences," Honda said; "My first film was about a woman diver [*The Blue Pearl*, 1951] which gave me a chance to deal with the relationship between humans and nature. That' a subject I think I'll never tire of" (Galbraith, *Monsters Are Attacking Tokyo* 59). Shigeru Kayama was also a motivated armchair naturalist. "As a boy, he had a great love for animals, including insects, but he was particularly fascinated with lizards and reptiles.... Even as he pursued a different path, studying economics at Hōsei University, he continued to read on his own about paleontology, geology, and ancient animals" (Angles, in Kayama 190).

Boss asks, "on Odo Island Godzilla is spoken of as a destructive monster of ancient legend ... what, then, is the relationship between the Godzilla which had just been created, or animated, within the post-atomic era and the Godzilla of Odo Island folklore" (103)? For Boss, too, the film leaves the tension between these two figurations of the monster unresolved. However, if we look closely at all the information Honda, Kayama, and Murata have provided us about the creature and its circumstances, including its visual representation, we can make better sense of their relationship. After exploring the mythic and spirit world roots of Gojira, let us now undertake the ironic work of rendering a supernatural creature natural.*

Part of the problem with "reading" *Gojira*, at least for English speaking audiences, is the unfortunate translation of a phrase from Dr. Yamane's report to the Diet committee after returning from his first encounter with the beast on Odo. This was one occasion when first impressions have indeed been lasting. In the dubbed American version, the paleontologist claims the beast was "resurrected by repeated experiments of H-bombs." In the original Japanese, Yamane says instead Gojira was "removed" from his habitat, that his abyssal environment was ruined, by those tests. This is an important distinction. "Resurrected" implies the monster was somehow reanimated, or perhaps re-awakened from its undersea slumber. Hence, we've all seen capsule reviews of the movie claiming he's been "brought back to life" or "roused from his long sleep." But however much comparisons with the

---

* Although the progressive enlargement of Godzilla from 1954 through his most recent iterations is beyond the scope of our discussion, Nathan J. Dominy and Ryan Carlsbeek published a fascinating article on the hypothetical "evolutionary pressures" which account for his original enormity and continued growth over the course of his film franchise in *Science* (May 2019).

VIII. Godzilla Ecology

restoration from its cryogenesis *The Beast from 20,000 Fathoms* may have influenced critics to interpret how the bomb tests brought us Gojira, our monster was not released from millions of years of icy suspension by atomic tests, nor had he been brumating interminably on the sea floor.

Yamane speculates just the opposite. He believes Godzilla has been living in a submerged habitat, a member of a species actively "reproducing itself" and "providing for its own survival and perhaps for others like it." He doubts if this creature is a lone survivor. The old paleontologist reiterates during the last moments of the film, "I can't believe Gojira was the last of its species." So, is he in fact a "two million year old monster" as the agitated reporter on his television tower informs his audience? If we accept that he is a member of a hidden race which has been reproducing itself, rather than a prehistoric revenant, he may well represent an ancient lineage, like coelacanths, crocodilians, or tuataras, but he needn't be very old himself. Considering him from an ecological as opposed to a mythopoetic perspective, he is probably nowhere near that ancient. At present the longest lived vertebrate species is believed to be the Greenland shark or eqallusuaq (*Somniosus microcephalus*), a large abyssal shark inhabiting Arctic waters. Marine biologists speculate it may live for 200–450 years. Keeping things seaworthy, the oldest whale species are the bowhead at about 200 years and the fin whale at 140 years. Like the Greenland shark, they are cold water denizens. On land, giant tortoises from Aldabra and the Galapagos Islands have lived as long as 188 years. Of the hypothetical ages of dinosaurs, in lieu of more research current estimates of their lifespans were surprisingly short. A recent exhibit at the American Museum of Natural History in New York speculated, based on available fossil evidence, *Tyrannosaurus rex* probably didn't live much longer than twenty to thirty years. Based on microscopic analysis of their joints, older specimens even suffered from arthritis and gout.

The paleontology related in the film is way out of date if not uninformed. By 1954 geologists and paleontologists already knew the Jurassic occurred much longer than only two million years ago. While Yamane says Gojira's species evolved from a marine reptile into a terrestrial animal during the Cretaceous period, on Odo Island he describes it as a "creature from the Jurassic age." He also traces the sand lodged in the shell of the trilobite found in Gojira's Odo Island footprint to undersea deposits of Jurassic strata. This is, one supposes, a contradiction with which we'll have to coexist. Regardless, if we accept Yamane's contention that Gojira is a member of a current but secretive species, we don't need to assume he is millions of years old. In keeping with his representation throughout the film, it would be more accurate to say he and his race are survivors but they are not relics. Yamane's Gojira is an apex predator. He inhabits a functional, or at least until recently functional, marine ecosystem whose fellow creatures forage and reproduce like any other organism.

Gojira represents one of the earliest films not only to warn about the dangers of nuclear testing from a human point of view, but also to warn about the damage we were doing from an ecocritical perspective. Honda and Murata appear to have been determined to present us with an encompassing vision of nuclear havoc at the environmental as well as the social level. As such, *Gojira* is not only one of the earliest admonitions against nuclear testing *per se*, but also among the earliest cinematic warnings about what it might be doing to our planetary ecosystems. Until Gojira emerged, we didn't know that his particular deep sea ecosystem was even there.

Inferentially, the Earth has its way of smacking us upside the head when we play fast and loose with her. In the case of this film the dangerous precedents we have set are limited to radiation and the violence of nuclear tests, but its cautionary stance establishes a precedent for later, more inclusive criticism of environmental backlash. In their book *Japan's Green Monsters*, Sean Rhoads and Brooke McCorkle explore the expanding ecocritical dimensions of the later films in the Godzilla franchise as well as of several other *kaiju* mainstays, like Biolante, in greater detail. In *Gojira* itself, though, radiophobia, as it swept through Japanese society in the wake of revelations about the long term effects of the atomic attacks, and more contemporaneously of the Lucky Dragon Five incident, is the form of its environmental concern.

Meanwhile the Odo Islanders, whose legend of the giant *kami* gave the beast its name, have always believed he was there. As the elder Izuma explains to Hagiwara while the official visitors attend the Island's ancient exorcism ceremony, a "terrifying monster" has appeared to the islanders before. Izuma functions as the unofficial historian, if not shamanic figure, of his community. The dismissal with which the younger islanders, notably the women, greet his conviction that the *kami* has returned infuriates him. "If you ridicule our traditions I'll feed you stupid cows to Gojira," he snaps.

Ironically enough, cows do seem to belong on Gojira's menu. Inada, headman of the community, informs Representative Oyama during his Diet committee testimony that a dozen of them, along with eight pigs, disappeared when Gojira trampled his village on that stormy night. Apparently the monster has cultivated a taste for beef and pork. In a deleted segment of the Hachiman Hill scene, the beast appears above the hilltop with a cow in his mouth, but Tsuburaya decided the cow was out of scale and the scene too gory, so it fell to the cutting room floor. I have to wonder if Steven Spielberg, a great fan of Japanese film, isn't paying backhanded homage to this deleted scene when his Tyrannosaurus appears above the tree line of its pen with a mouthful of goat in *Jurassic Park*.

Hunger Games

In any case our monster's excursions ashore appear to be foraging expeditions; he isn't just being a tourist. David Kalat argues Godzilla "is not hungry" (48) and his assaults on Tokyo aren't "motivated," that his malevolence is gratuitous, and this is precisely the most horrifying aspect of his attack (47–48). I don't entirely dismiss that observation insofar as there seems to be no reason for his violence from the perspective of those hard luck Japanese who get in his way. On the other hand, from our perspective as film viewers gifted with what the Russian literary critic Mikhail Bakhtin described as "an excess of seeing and knowing" by comparison with the film's characters, we can simultaneously comprehend their terror while understanding the beast may be looking for a meal after all.

Shigeru Kayama's "G" story tells of "a giant sea monster which comes on land to feed on a remote island's cattle before finally attacking Tokyo." Kayama's story concentrated on the creature's "voracious appetite" (Brothers, *Atomic Dreams* 23). His predation of the Odo Island livestock follows the author's original depiction. The old fisherman Izuma also tells Hagiwara that Gojira will come ashore and eat people after he's eaten "all the fish in the sea." With due respect to the venerable Izuma, nothing in the film bears out his concerns. Gojira is not a filter feeder, like a baleen whale or a basking shark. He hasn't got the equipment for it. Regardless, unlike the *Beast from 20,000 Fathoms*, who gulps a hapless New York City cop, or even King Kong, who chews on a native after escaping from his stockade, we never see him eating humans, only frying them with his radioactive aerosol or squashing them, as when he steps on the train he's just derailed in the Shinagawa yards. He's too big to benefit from a human meal; it would be like eating a chocolate sprinkle.* Pigs, though, inhabit the lower size range of his culinary interests.

At the Diet hearing (no translinguistic pun intended) Inada reports nine islanders killed. Cattle "disappear" from Odo but apparently not people. No one wants to be crushed or irradiated but fear of being eaten is not a present issue in this film. Furthermore, the disappearance of the fish population around Odo would also explain Gojira's checking out Tokyo Bay for alternative sources of nutrition, even if the Japanese coast guard's depth bombing just off the mouth of the bay hadn't driven him there. During his initial foray through the Shinagawa rail yards he famously picks up a commuter coach in his mouth, then spits it out. It's big enough to catch his attention—especially after smashing into his foot—but this, he concludes, will be a barren source of nourishment.

According to Izuma, Gojira traditionally announces his advent to the islanders by ruining their catch whereupon they would sacrifice a young girl on a raft to keep the monster from coming ashore and eating them, too. Notwithstanding the legendary problem of man-eating, this tradition as the old man relates it, in conjunction with the nuclear nexus, tells us some important things about our monster. For one thing, Gojira likely isn't all that fond of coming ashore in the first place. Accustomed to having his bulk supported by buoyancy when submerged, and his appetite satisfied by large sea life, he needs to adjust to being out of the water. If in fact his size and bulk has been amplified by nuclear radiation, that would impact his agility and cut down on the number of types of sea life he could catch.†

---

* Shigeru Kayama's 1955 novelization depicts the creature snatching a young girl off the top of Hachiman Hill, possibly to lend credence to Izuma's tale of maiden sacrifice in ancient times.

† In Takashi Yamazaki's 2023 reboot *Godzilla Minus One*, we see the originally T-Rex–sized Godzilla being irradiated by the Crossroads atomic bomb test, and when next we encounter him several months later, he has swollen to five times his original size.

VIII. Godzilla Ecology

In both cases when we see him actually rising out of Tokyo Bay, just before his brief Shinagawa escapade and then prior to his all-out assault on Tokyo, he wobbles side to side—motion which Akira Ifukube's halting, lower-register accompaniment emphasizes—and splashes with his arms, as though negotiating his balance. A few nights before that, when he rises for a looksee and terrifies the revelers on the party boat, his head and neck slump and he quickly submerges again. We're watching him deal with leaving his primary habitat.

Each of his ventures ashore lasts a bit longer than the last, culminating in his extended rampage through Tokyo. He also appears to be mostly nocturnal, rising out of the sea during the daytime only twice but briefly. Once, preceding his Hachiman Hill appearance, in the original take of the scene he snatches a cow, and at the end of the film he sounds to howl his death agony before sinking back into the bay and disintegrating.

That the monster can't seem to find much to eat is inflected throughout the film. As mentioned, the scene of Gojira rising up behind Hachiman Hill on Odo Island with a cow in his mouth was cut from the final version because Honda and Tsuburaya didn't think the cow scaled properly. In fact throughout the film *no one eats*. We may assume the human characters are eating something, sometime, just as the missing Odo Island cattle infer the monster ate them, but we are never allowed to see it. Emiko serves her father a tray of beverages but even this service is thwarted by the sirens and symbolic footfalls announcing Gojira's arrival. The Odo Island fisherman can't catch anything to eat either. Their legend may hold that when Gojira eats all the fish in the sea he will come ashore and eat people, but we understand he's not equipped to go chasing tuna, salmon or mackerel. The fishing is bare because his radioactivity is so toxic, or because his sheer size and the turbulence around him as he moves underwater has frightened the fish away.

This meme of fasting even extends to *Godzilla, King of the Monsters*. Serizawa has to turn down Steve Martin's suggestion they have dinner that evening because Emiko is coming to his house to tell him "something important." And behind this pervasive fast lies the memory of both the near starvation facing Japan at the end of the Pacific War, and the great contaminated fish immolation caused by the Lucky Dragon episode and resulting radiophobic panic.

Since he is an abyssal organism, his tiny eyes and aversion to light make adaptive sense, and his landward excursions, even at night, are relatively brief. It also makes sense that they become a little longer as he gets hungrier. His visits to Odo Island last for only a few minutes, he returns to the bay shortly after his initial foray into Shinagawa, and even his protracted excursion through Tokyo lasts barely fifteen minutes onscreen. This may not be in real time but he still doesn't dawdle on land. The reason, from our ecological perspective, is indeed that he's lost in an alien habitat, plus it is loud, bright, painful, and confusing. Part also, allowing for the protracted metaphor of Gojira the nuclear text, is his ability to inflict incomprehensible damage within a short time. Nevertheless, given these difficulties, hunger is the most logical reason a giant with so many adjustments to make would finally lurch ashore.

Travels with Gojira

In his testimony before the Diet committee Yamane poses the question of why Godzilla should appear in Japanese territorial waters. He partially answers by blaming hydrogen bomb testing. However, the creature's appearances since antiquity—or, to extend Dr. Yamane's contention, perhaps the emergence of others like him—indicate it wasn't only the bomb tests in the distant Pacific which chased him Japanward. More likely, given his or his ancestors' appearances to the islanders in the past, the waters around Odo Island *represent a traditional point on his species' migratory feeding route.*

Humpback whales, for example, follow the long western Pacific trenches along the Ogasawara Islands and the coast of Japan to and from their Arctic feeding areas. Male sperm whales (hello again, Moby Dick) migrate between their feeding grounds in the Sea of Okhotsk and their breeding grounds off Indonesia and the Philippines, passing directly by and through the Izu Archipelago. Viewed in this way, the idea of a predator following its prey on a seasonal basis resolves one of the film's unstated conundrums, namely, what Gojira is doing in Japanese waters when his usual habitation is so far to the south. Let's have a closer look at his peregrination as suggested by Dr. Yamane's analysis of what happened to him.

VIII. Godzilla Ecology

Beginning in 1946,* the U.S. conducted a series of tests of various designs for both atomic and hydrogen bombs in the Pacific. The outer Marshall Islands atolls of Kwajalein, Eniwetok and Bikini, the latter used for the Castle Bravo test which contaminated the fishing boat Daigyo Fukuryu Maru (Lucky Dragon Five) in March 1954, are approximately 2,400 miles south-southeast of Japan. Incidentally, this was roughly the same area where Moby Dick, enraged at being harpooned by Ahab's crew, rammed and sank the whaleship *Pequod* to conclude his eponymous narrative. The region is just a bad place to infuriate leviathans of all sorts. Our monster, then, has traveled a long way to arrive at Odo and, eventually, Tokyo Bay where he would meet his fate. Given the time frame of the film, released in November 1954, the Marshalls are the likeliest sites where Godzilla suffered exposure to American nuclear tests.

From an ecological perspective the nuclear tests might well have sickened or deformed Gojira, a bigger subject we'll return to below. However, they would only have had to destroy his local foraging area, wiping out or scattering the cetaceans, giant squid or large sharks on which he normally fed, to set him in motion along his natural feeding paths, bringing him proximate to the Japanese coastline. Moby Dick wasn't particular to the region but a migratory forager as well. The Marshall Islands had been a favored seasonal hunting ground of 19th-century whalers who arrived there when they knew their quarry would. Moreover, these islands lie near the southeastern end of a chain of deep sea trenches including the Bougainville, Mariana, Izu Bonin, and Japan Trenches, which stretch in an arc all the way to, and beyond, the Japanese coastline. Perhaps not coincidentally, the Izu Archipelago is a favored feeding area for sperm whales annually migrating north from their wintering area near the Marshall Islands, lending substance to the notion Gojira and his fellow behemoths would have followed their food source to the Izus even without thermonuclear coercion. The Izu Bonin trench, especially, passes by the Izu Islands, the archipelago of which Odo Island is at least a close outlier. Such abyssal pathways could handily guide a gigantic marine organism between its far flung Pacific basin feeding grounds.

---

* The two Crossroads atomic bomb tests—Able and Baker—on July 1 and July 25, 1946, are central to Takashi Yamazaki's *Godzilla Minus One*. One of the tests—most likely Baker, which was set off underwater—is shown irradiating the submerged Godzilla and beginning his transition into a giant radioactive kaiju.

In Search of Godzilla

As for that persistent, if mordant, question of why Gojira would show up in Tokyo Bay at all, especially if he was inured to deep sea habitats, the Izu-Bonin arc, a system of submarine ridges paralleling the Sagami Trough to the north and west of the Izu Archipelago, runs directly from these islands to the mouth of Tokyo Bay. We learn from the newscast watched by Yamane, Emiko, Shinkichi and Ogata that the frigate fleet will attack the monster to the west of Odo. This is in fact where the Izu-Bonin arc intersects with the Sagami Trench. Thus, it would represent a submarine route Gojira could follow directly to the mouth of the Bay, especially if Japanese Coast Guard frigates were pestering him with depth charges closer to Odo Island itself.

Nor need we assume of an ocean basin riven with miles deep trenches and other vast seabed landforms our Gojira species (which I'm tempted to christen *Godzilla yamanensis*; monograph pending) was native to only one region proximate enough to Bikini Atoll for the Crossroads and Castle shots to irradiate him. Nor would it require nuclear testing to set these submarine behemoths in motion. One may speculate such disturbances as the monumental eruptions along the Ring of Fire of Taupo in AD 232, Krakatau in 536 and 1883, or Tambora in 1815, not to mention periodic undersea eruptions all along the Ring, would have chased off Gojira's and his predecessors' large food sources, sending others of his species on abyssal feeding migrations.

Conveniently, the vast arc of submarine trenches would point the way north whether the imperatives were annual feeding migrations or environmental disturbances. The islands of Japan were already populated thousands of years ago and these scenarios would account, however euhemeristically, for the appearances of Gojira's predecessors in the earliest traditions of the Odo Islanders. Kalat asserts that the Odo Island natives have never seen the monster themselves, making their legends "frighteningly prescient" (49).

I would argue that though members of his species might not have presented themselves to this generation of Odo Islanders, the legends, ancient as they are, indicate members of his race have indeed shown up there in the past. Gojira himself is a nuclear blast damaged and mutated example of his type, so his behavior may not be entirely characteristic. What's more, though we've covered this issue above, the islanders' keeping the exorcism dance alive in their isolated culture, while the young women reject their tradition, plays to the film's

VIII. Godzilla Ecology

all-important contrast between Japan's ancient ways and emerging consumerist ethos.

The Odo tradition, at least insofar as Izuma relates it, never mentions Gojira's toxic breath, radioactive or otherwise. When he delivers his conclusions to the Diet committee, Professor Yamane as yet doesn't suspect it, or at least hasn't considered how the creature sank all those merchant and fishing ships. Irradiation by the Bravo shot and other bomb tests most likely account for Gojira's nuclear capability so the creature's ancestors just as likely wouldn't have possessed it in its incendiary form. However, many organisms, including stink bugs, vinegarroons, archerfish, and spitting cobras can eject venom or other fluids when either defending themselves or hunting. Perhaps Gojira's radioactive breath was, before exposure to the bomb, a corrosive or toxic discharge (which mythological dragons in the Chinese and Japanese traditions possessed), used by his species for self-defense, in territorial combat with other Gojiras, or for intoxicating and stunning large prey.

Whatever else he may be, our monster isn't fast on his feet. His hands aren't webbed. His tail isn't vertically compressed, like a marine iguana's or a crocodile's, which means he probably can't swim very well. To hinder or cripple a whale or giant squid long enough to catch it, he would need some feeding technique to slow it down. One can imagine him spraying his venom upward at whales near the surface or into the faces of abyssal squid to stop them cold or poison them sufficiently for him to seize them in his claws or mouth. Gamma rays from the nuclear bomb tests likely turned this natural discharge radioactive, just as they have affected the creature generally and turned him into an immense walking meltdown.

We only see Gojira employ his radioactive breath for two reasons: to sink ships and to defend himself when he senses threats from his terrestrial surroundings. There's nothing gratuitous about his violence, since he only resorts to it on land once enraged by artillery fire and high voltage electricity. "We were the ones responsible for triggering Godzilla's violence," asserts actor Akira Takarada, who played Ogata (cited in Brothers 2015:161). He is correct in both the narrative's generalities and particulars.

Nor is it difficult to imagine a marine organism in hunting mode, equipped with this instinctive capability to envenomate, mistaking a large vessel overhead for a cetacean. Watching him trying to bite into

In Search of Godzilla

the railroad coach in the Shinagawa yard and then dropping it, it's also not difficult to imagine him grabbing ahold of a sinking ship and spitting it out with the same frustration. After bringing down ship after ship and finding them all inedible, is it surprising he would finally surface on Odo where he could secure some food? Given he'd been incinerating boats for what must have been at least a few weeks and getting nowhere, it took some time for him to wax hungry enough to haul his bulk ashore.

Interestingly enough, after his forays onto Odo Island where on both occasions he helps himself to the Islanders' livestock, we don't hear anything more about Gojira's sinking ships. He attacks neither Dr. Yamane's research vessel nor the Coast Guard frigates which are bombarding him. Nor does he blast the navy vessel floating directly above him as it delivers Ogata, Serizawa, and the oxygen destroyer into his very lap. A full belly apparently does wonders for Gojira's disposition. Being primarily nocturnal, it's also possible he doesn't strike at ships in daylight.

Ashore in Tokyo, Gojira continues to behave like a forager. Like many modern reptiles, we only see him chomping down on things that *move*, a meme Steven Spielberg exploited in the first *Jurassic Park* when paleontologist Alan Grant warns his companions not to budge after the Tyrannosaurus breaks out of its enclosure. Ashore, Gojira transitions to an animal defending itself as any living organism under attack would. He is quick enough to catch cows and pigs on Odo but, unfortunately, the Tokyo conurbation was thin on cattle even in 1954. About the only thing big enough to interest him would have been the train that hit his foot whose movement would have attracted him, or the retreating tanks of the hapless 49th Armored Division he fries after they shell him at point-blank range.

Whereas neither artillery nor high voltage electricity are enough to kill him, that's not to say they don't hurt. His first use of his corrosive breath as a defense is against the electrical towers which have seared him. When later he steps on catenary wires above a rail line, he roars angrily and lashes his tail. Thereafter he retaliates, not mindlessly as some critics have claimed, but as a precaution against an environment which seems to threaten pain at every turn. A moment after cooking the tanks, he peers over some rooftops and spots a police car which looks suspicious enough to merit another a prophylactic gust of bad breath.

VIII. Godzilla Ecology

When Gojira unleashes his radioactive breath, his dorsal fins illuminate. Earlier, we discussed the monster's identity with the primal marine dragon deity of ancient Japan, Ryujin, whose name, you will recall, means *luminous being*. In addition to this mythopoetic allusiveness, from our biological perspective we could attribute his glow to other causes. His radioactivity is one likely stimulus for this effect but I think there's another, richer, dimension to it. Many deep sea organisms have bioluminescent properties. Bioluminescence serves numerous purposes in the lightless depths of the sea including the attraction of mates, the attraction of prey, and territorial warning.

Most of these organisms contain specialized bodies of luciferin, a family of organic compounds which produce light when oxidized by their basal enzyme, luciferase. Under certain circumstances, which vary by species but include agitation, the luciferous organism produces the needed amount of luciferase to galvanize the oxidation process. Lantern fish of the genus *Diaphus* can light up their entre bellies as well as their noses. Anglerfish (*Lophius* or *Melanocetus*) carry modified bioluminescent barbels on their upper jaws to attract prey organisms to their mouths. In some cases these creatures symbiotically carry discrete bioluminescent microorganisms in specialized cell bodies; in others, they carry vesicles of luciferin within their own cellular structures.

In Gojira's case, the luciferin-bearing cells are apparently located in his dorsal fins, and deployment of his venom activates manufacture of luciferase in those structures which illuminates them. Thus, we may speculate his bioluminescence is linked both to feeding and defensive behaviors. His angry reaction to the brightly lit Wako Department Store clock tower, which he smashes, and to searchlights or flashbulbs, which enrage him, are also indicative of an animal to whom bioluminescence engenders a range of natural stimuli. It might also be linked to mating behavior, since finding a mate in the pitchblende world he normally inhabits can't be easy. Either way, the effect is spectacular.

Another remarkable aspect of his dorsal profile is how jagged it is. Unlike the ovular dorsal plates of the Stegosaurs, to which various critics have compared them, his look like they were tortured out of his back, or perhaps deformed by the nuclear blast or blasts to which he has been subjected. I suspect Honda and Murata, with input from their design staff, meant to suggest the stegosaurs as another Jurassic planform for comparison with Gojira by having a large replica skeleton occupy such

In Search of Godzilla

a prominent place on the desk in Professor Yamane's study. This idea might be more convincing if Gojira's tail featured a thagomizer, but few attributes in nature are gratuitous. Given the power of his tail such a structure would only be a nuisance. Most paleontologists now believe the stegosaurs' dorsal plates helped the animal regulate its body temperature (an idea that resurfaces in the much later film *Shin Gojira*) but a marine creature wouldn't have much use for such a system of thermal regulation. Another way to think of such dramatic castellation involves mating behavior; perhaps the more pronounced and ragged the dorsal profile, especially when lit up by his bioluminescence, the more effective a sexual attractant they would be.

I've saved consideration of our monster's most striking feature for last. Gojira lacks a consistent attribute of large marine organisms, all of whom have slick or relatively smooth skin to minimize friction and ease their movement through the water. Pinnipeds, too, have tightly napped fur. We don't know what he looked like before suffering exposure to those nuclear blasts, but we do know he had no large scales or scutes, or other forms of armor plating on his body. His later representation, with more alligator or caiman lizard like skin, was an attribute of the Toho sequels and need not concern us here. We also know what keloid scarring looks like.

He is not necessarily a reptile, since recent paleontology tells us many active dinosaurs had skeletal capillary saturation closer to warm-blooded species. Gojira has survived in the very low temperatures and high pressure in his native habitat. Most likely, then, he was originally covered with tough but smooth, insulated flesh with fatty layers comparable to a cetacean's. The glistening skin of Charles Knight's Brontosaurus in its lacustrine paradise also comes to mind. Part of Gojira's "incredible powers of survival," as Yamane put it to the security officials, would surely be attributable to having evolved to withstand the vicissitudes of those depths.

Much of the brunt of the heat, concussion and gamma ray saturation from the Castle Bravo and other nuclear tests was absorbed by the water, but enough of it reached Gojira to burn and irradiate him. It is also possible at least some of his surface deformities, especially around his face, are cancerous. Resilient as he is, Gojira may be in pain from his burns, which also might account for all the howling he does. Is it, then, any coincidence he spends relatively little time ashore when he

VIII. Godzilla Ecology

does surface, since the water may be more soothing to his burns than the air?

Modern paleontology has reconfigured the meat eating dinosaur from our old Charles Knight–era hulking pea-brain to quick thinking predator. Honda and Murata were a few decades ahead of the field. Though critics have argued for the irrationality or mindlessness of the monster's behavior, even he, like the film in which he is a central player, is not so simple. His reactions to his environment suggest, in fact, that he possesses a feral inwardness. On several occasions Gojira regards his surroundings thoughtfully, as when he first approaches the protective barrier of electric towers, pauses, and looks back and forth as though considering what to do. During his catastrophic excursion through Tokyo, he also pauses several times to ponder where he is and where to go next. When he approaches the Wako Department Store Hattori tower whose clock faces he perceives as baleful eyes, he snarls a challenge before embracing the structure, destroying it.*

The scene of Gojira's exit from Tokyo is a master class in collaborative composition wherein the cinematographic skills of Masao Tamai, the effects planning of Eiji Tsuburaya, and the directorial genius of Ishiro Honda seamlessly converge. In a distance shot, we see iconography in action: Gojira wading down the Sumidagawa, silhouetted against a background of flames which limn his saurian mass with a pulsing sheen. Roaring as though feeling blocked or even trapped by the inferno he initiated, he clearly isn't enjoying it; he has had quite enough, *olegato gozaymas*, of being machinegunned, bombed, shelled, electrocuted, rammed by trains, and blinded by searchlights. And Tokyo, judging by the way the dockside spectators cheer on the Sabre jets rocketing him throughout his departure, has had quite enough of him, too.

As when he first emerged from the bay this abyssal leviathan tests his balance, waving his arms before him to stabilize himself while unsupported by his natural buoyancy. On his way back to the bay he stops to consider the best way to remove the barrier of the Kachidoki Bridge over the Sumida River before grabbing the eastern span and

---

* This was actually an important scene for more than just its spectacle. According to Carrozza, this Tokyo landmark, about 160 feet high, predetermined Gojira's size, since effects supervisor Eiji Tsuburaya specifically wanted him to be big enough to attack it (72). The effect we get is that he perceives it as a rival creature whose bright eyes are staring him down.

flipping it into the harbor. In a dramatic scene compensatory of the distant perspective on his exit thus far, we see the tidal surge caused by the fallen bridge as it picks up boats along the harbor and hurls them against their wharves. He is now free to return to the bay after another fruitless sojourn ashore to serve his appetite.

Gojira's teratogenicity also serves a critical function in both political and aesthetic terms. Teratology had been naturalized by Darwin as an aspect of natural selection, as something which could prove either disadvantageous, for example in the Precambrian extinction, or advantageous, as in the evolution of feathers in dinosaurs as thermoregulators, later predicating the emergence of birds and flight. Teratogenicity caused by irradiation from nuclear bombs de-naturalized the teratogenic, and among his many other symbolic attributions Gojira symbolized that reversed process.

Godzilla Geology

I've speculated—and reviewed the speculation of others—that there is something quintessentially Japanese about our monster such that when disenfranchised from his national and cultural origins he becomes a mannequin of sorts. Here, I'd like to consider how his form and behavior also inflects the Japanese land itself.

A cursory look at her landforms suggests the island nation was literally tortured into existence. Her northeast island of Hokkaido and the northeastern half of Honshu, her main island, sit astride a narrow curving arm of the North American tectonic plate, sometimes referred to as the Okhotsk plate. The southwestern half of Honshu, all of Shikoku and Kyushu, are located near the eastern edge of the Eurasian plate. A small wedge of Honshu near Shizuoka lies on the northeastern tip of the Philippine Sea plate, which is driving northwestward like a wedge. The vast Pacific plate lies not far offshore to the east where the North American plate arm overrides and slowly swallows the subducting Pacific Plate as it grinds westward. Caught between all these shifting land and seafloor masses, Japan stress fractures longitudinally along its Median Tectonic Line which runs through much of Honshu, the Inland Sea, and Kyushu. Some of this fault line is so deep that its location can only be speculated. Catastrophic earthquakes, volcanism, and tsunamis are woven through

VIII. Godzilla Ecology

Japan's history ancient and modern; it would only be natural for these events to have inspired her vast crèche of spirits, monsters, dragons, demons, and baleful chthonic deities.

Moreover, these conditions formed the character of the Japanese people. They had to be tough and resilient to reconstruct their settlements and their lives over and over, and the constant feudal wars that shaped her political life, of which the Pacific War was the final turn of the martial wheel, also contributed to shaping their defiant nature. They also had to be imaginative to conceptualize the powers nature hurled against them into meaningful, even hopeful narratives of gods and heroes in order to make symbolic sense of the capriciousness of their land. Those thunderous footfalls of the approaching kaiju, audible even before he rose from the sea or the harbor, must have joined in a composite of earthquakes, exploding calderas, thunderclaps, the thud of falling bombs growing closer. Gojira became an amalgam of Japanese history and Japanese destiny at once.

As a natural disaster in his own right, Gojira represents—in addition to everything else he symbolizes—Japan's long history of suffering tectonic and volcanic upheavals. He is consistent with its geological character in his destructiveness as well as in his abyssal origins. Observers of the Myōjin-shō eruptions watched as crests of black lava rose from the sea, releasing gouts of steam, then sank beneath the water again. Films and photos of these events were spread by newsreel and newspaper all over Japan. The spectacle of Gojira with his jagged back, struggling to rise out of Tokyo Bay at night, must have reminded audiences of nothing so much as this seismic phenomenon. Judging from the prominent mention of the volcanic disaster of 1952 by the Coast Guard officer trying to explain the disappearance of the *Eiko Maru* early in *Gojira*, it was an impression the Japanese still husbanded so that as they watched the film it must have composted in their imaginations with the Castle Bravo irradiation of the Lucky Dragon Five.

IX

The Science Fiction Rhetoric of *Gojira*

SO WHAT KIND OF MOVIE DO we call *Gojira*? If you thought that would be the easy part, think again. We have discussed several genres including horror, documentary, social or political commentary and even mythographic representation, but always prominently including "monster movie." One elusive category, "science fiction," keeps peeking in and hiding behind a welter of alternate definitions. To clarify this bedeviling issue of genre, we might profitably turn to Brian McHale's concept of the dominant, the organizing concept behind the *membra disjuncta* of any narrative. According to McHale in his landmark critical study *Postmodernist Fiction* (1987), the dominant of a postmodernist work is ontological—that is, what world is this? What principles govern the functioning of reality here? Although McHale is not directly addressing science fiction, we can utilize his insight regarding an organizing principle to understand how science fiction as a genre, and *Gojira* in particular, uses its particular slant on the various worlds it represents to rewire its connection between its world and the one it purportedly represents.

In this view, McHale intersects with science fiction author and critic Stanisław Lem who considers how the core of a science fiction story is a strange or alien phenomenon whose alterity sets it apart from the mundane world while at the same time "Only the outer shell of this world is formed by the strange phenomena; the inner core has a solid nonfantastic meaning" (42). Gojira himself, viewed as decentralized for the moment, is the "strange phenomen[on]" while that inner reality is Japan's complex, lingering angst about the late Pacific War. Lem continues, "As in life we can solve real problems with the help of images of nonexistent beings, so in literature [as in film—RW] can we signal

IX. The Science Fiction Rhetoric of *Gojira*

the existence of real problems with the help of prima facie impossible occurrences or objects. Even when the happenings it describes are totally impossible, a science-fiction work may still point out meaningful, indeed rational, problems" (43).

To complicate this issue a bit more, *Gojira* premiered at a time when science fiction was burgeoning in popularity. Many, in fact, look back at the period of the late 1940s–mid 1950s as a golden age of the genre. The atom had been split. Man had usurped the authentic power for universal destruction previously reserved in cultural lore to the Deity. When, in the classic science fiction film *The Day the Earth Stood Still* (1951), Professor Barnhardt questions the alien visitor Klaatu if he possesses the power to destroy the Earth, Klaatu replies, "I assure you such a power exists." We must recall it had only been six years since Hiroshima and Nagasaki and the film is taking advantage of mankind's continuing incredulity about what we had already unleashed.

Nature had ceased to behave rationally, and rational explanations of its irrational behavior were beyond the ken of those untrained in the esoteric language of advanced mathematics—in other words, practically anyone without a degree in physics. As Robert Adams put it, "To describe the SF published in the 1940s and 1950s as Golden Age is—obviously—not to use a neutral or value-free description. Coined by a partisan fandom, the phrase valorizes a particular sort of writing: hard SF, linear narratives, heroes solving problems or countering threats in a space-operatic or a technological-adventure idiom" (287). It also valorizes a privileged understanding of difficult concepts and arcane capabilities like controlled nuclear fission and the emergence of atomic medicine.

Science fiction as a genre has, until the past few decades, struggled up a critical salmon ladder to achieve the legitimacy that makes a book like this one even possible. Carl Freedman, writing about the literary genre of science fiction, has insisted that "all genuine critique must expect such conservative resistance, and even the faintest suspicion that science fiction has been keeping such dangerous theoretical company may be enough to motivate the belittling and ghettoization that science fiction generally suffers at the hands of those who exercise great influence in literary matters" (86). Freedman's warning echoes the comments of Julio Cortázar, whom I cited in my introduction, that science fiction and horror were considered lowbrow entertainment. Despite this disregard,

In Search of Godzilla

Science fiction embraced the geological and evolutionary timescales of nineteenth-century science and began to think of the planet as something that preceded our species and could conceivably continue without us. Such conceptualizations of the planet as a changeable environment turned the tradition of apocalyptic fiction toward mundane visions of environmental catastrophe instead of divine judgment [Vint 117–119].

Operating under the radar, so to speak, science fiction was rewiring the discussion, if not the comprehension, of what the world was or could really be about. By the time it emerged as a legitimate artistic vision of its time, its time was already waiting for it. As Stanisław Lem put it,

> It is the premise of science fiction that anything shown shall in principle be interpretable empirically and rationally. In science fiction there can be no inexplicable marvels, no transcendences, no devils or demons—and the pattern of occurrences must be verisimilar. Even when the happenings it describes are totally impossible, a science-fiction work may still point out meaningful, indeed rational, problems [42–43].

Gojra and Japanese Colonialism

Influential Hungarian critic and theorist Georg Lukács developed his idea that narrative fiction, the novel in particular, evolved as western civilization became more dominantly capitalist, bourgeois, and, at the same time, necessarily colonialist. Critics of science fiction, following his lead, discovered inferences of the colonial mentality in the late evolving genre. The occupation of other planets, inhabited or uninhabited, the synthetic production of intelligent life forms like androids or cyborgs to act as laborers and servants, the mining and exploitation of outerworldly mineral resources, and ultimately the formation of "galactic empires" suited perfectly Lukács' model. "The constitutive relationship between colonialism and sf creates both problems and opportunities," notes Vint (62).

In what ways might *Gojira* reflect a consciousness of, or fear of, or response to, colonialism? Well, any film that invokes the late Pacific War as consistently—let us say, pervasively—as this one does is of necessity invoking that war's colonialist essential nature. Since Japan had been only recently east Asia's foremost colonial power, did *Gojira* appear to have a retributive aspect? For a brief time—just a couple of

IX. The Science Fiction Rhetoric of Gojira

decades—her reach extended from Sakhalin in the north (though also, briefly, to the central Aleutian Islands), to Malaysia and Indonesia to the south. It encompassed most of coastal China, Formosa, the Philippines, Indochina, and realistically threatened Ceylon, India, and Australia. During this period Japan ejected from Asia as well as impersonated the European powers she had long admired and envied. In the process, her armed forces earned a reputation for criminal brutality.

Gojira's emergence from the ruins of the war was also, therefore, an emergence from the wreckage of colonial overextension. That under the imposed MacArthur constitution she would very quickly commit herself to a purely commercial domination of east Asia, building a formidable manufacturing sector and a merchant marine to import raw materials and distribute her products, conforms to the irony of Gojira announcing himself by attacking and effectively crippling her maritime commerce. Within a few weeks the country orders its shipping lanes closed. By making a point of this, the film also gestures to the economic strangulation it experienced during the last year of the war, when allied submarines ranged through the Sea of Japan and the East China Sea, and even managed to shut off the Bongo Strait.

Gojira's Complex Rhetoric of Past and Future

Gojira is science fiction in most of these aforementioned senses but it subverts its own forward looking demeanor when it bemoans the way the past keeps catching up with Japan. This is indicative that at the time of the making of *Gojira* recent history was, to paraphrase James Joyce, a nightmare from which Japan seemed unable to awaken. The power grid hastily jointed together and arrayed against Gojira is, for example, an attempt at replicating on local scale Japan's old jerrybuilt power grid, and holding *on* to the past. That the Japanese unleash all the available branches of their defense forces—naval, artillery, armor, air force—also feels like the nation is testing the limits of its pacifistic postwar constitution.

We can rephrase Freedman in cinematic terms to argue that *Gojira* and, indeed, the kaiju genre, has self-isolated with a stylistic vocabulary distinct unto itself. Whatever else it alludes to, and whatever else it signifies, *Gojira* is a science fiction film. This genre establishes

In Search of Godzilla

a characteristic rhetoric through which it relates its story. According to the Croatian critic Darko Suvin, science fiction is "a literary genre whose necessary and sufficient conditions are the presence and interaction of estrangement and cognition, and whose main formal device is an imaginative framework alternative to the author's empirical environment" (qtd. in Freedman 16). Suvin adds that estrangement "differentiates [science fiction] from the 'realistic' literary mainstream," while cognition differentiates it from myth, the folk tale, and fantasy (Freedman 16).

Estrangement, the impossibility of a gigantic prehistoric monster impervious to modern weaponry, is an evident quality of *Gojira*. However, it becomes problematic to classify the film according to Suvin's categories* because, as we have shown, it bodies forth so much mythic content that the degree to which "cognition" can differentiate it from myth is self-limited. In another, somewhat simpler, categorization of the genre, Aeon Skoble asserts, "I take science fiction to be that branch of literature (and by extension films) that deals with the effects of science or technology on the human condition or that explores the human condition via science" (91).

In *Gojira* the impact of technology is Janus-faced: nuclear bomb testing mutates and sickens a Lazarus taxon, compelling it to the surface and heaving it against civilization, while a related form of technology, Serizawa's oxygen destroyer, brings the monster's rampage to an end. The film even more deeply explores the impact of science on the human condition in the anguished conflict between conscience and curiosity as variously illustrated by the reactions of Yamane and Serizawa to the emergence of Gojira.

Still other critics have seized on the historicizing aspect of science fiction as "a genre whose origins are inextricably linked to science becoming culturally dominant in Western cultures during the late nineteenth and early twentieth centuries" (Vint 3). Certainly, *Gojira* conforms to this idea by presenting two scientists, Yamane and Serizawa, as dominant figures in the newly disrupted Japanese culture. It is to Yamane the government turns for explication of the creature's appearance and

---

* Suvin's generic categories, like Freedman's observations, are addressed specifically to science fiction literature. We are invoking critical license here to extend their critiques to film.

powers, whereas Yamane himself turns to Tanabe for explication of its radioactive properties. But it is to Serizawa that all turn for deliverance by way of his cutting edge experiments with the frangibility of the water molecule. All the other characters—government officials, military officers, journalists, and principal laymen like Ogata and Emiko—valorize these men of science as, they hope, their deliverers.

On the other hand, as already discussed, the commitment to empiricism of both Yamane and Serizawa is, as it were, x-rayed by the screenplay to locate the point at which empiricism overturns into sociopathy and humanistic viewpoints become irrelevant to curiosity for its own sake. The film seems to suggest that a superflux of misery needs to accumulate before the suffering that results from the misapplication of technology outweighs the imperatives of discovery.

On the other hand, Honda and Tsuburaya are painstaking in their determination to make their monster's depredations of Tokyo as realistic as possible and thereby to valorize the role of cognition in the reception of their film. Where does *Gojira* operate in terms of cognition? When the fictitious monster destroys recognizable Tokyo landmarks like the Wako Department Store clock tower or the Kachidoki Bridge, he roots himself in day to day reality, as if striving to contest, or at least minimize, his own unreality. The moment such landmarks become identifiable, they amplify, if just for a moment, the sense that what we are watching is really happening.

Hachiman Hill Sequence

Xavier Aldana Reyes has extensively studied visual and auditory triggers in horror film. His comments here are particularly relevant to Gojira's big reveal during the Hachiman Hill sequence on Odo Island about 22 minutes into the film:

> The startle effect or the "jump scare" is, quite easily, the most prevalent somatic effect encouraged and exploited by Horror ... the actual object that causes the startle ... is not normally enough to startle on its own because the effect does not work representationally but somatically. Although not all scenes of dread lead to a startle, they often do, so the startle is normally preceded by a period of anticipation and heightening of emotions that increases the chances of a strong physiological reaction [151].

In Search of Godzilla

Reyes further adds, "Whilst the moment leading up to the reveal, where it is signposted or prefigured, is still invested in the intradiegesis of the film, that where the viewer may be shocked by the image is not" (153). In the Hachiman Hill scene Gojira rears up slowly, looks down the hillside and then roars towards his left. As has been noted earlier, in the original filming of this scene the creature first appears chewing on a cow. Deleting that scene makes it necessary to cut back to the faces of Yamane and the villagers as they watch this monstrous form rising above the crest of the hill. So, this was a fortuitous cut, which delays for a few seconds more anticipation of what the creature looks like. However when he leans over the hilltop and roars down at Emiko, eyes glaring, and she screams back, Gojira directly assaults the viewer who empathetically sees him, closing in, through Emiko's eyes.

Aldana Reyes notes, "The viewer's experience of extreme moments of engagement, such as that of witnessing torture or corporeal harm ... places the body at the centre of critical attention at the representational, emotional and affective levels" (9). It is a powerful demonstration of Honda's craftsmanship. So, too, is Honda's refusal to frame the creature over Emiko's shoulders leaving us unsure of just how close he is to her. We're left to imagine his proximity, but we are also guided in forming our impression by the fact that she's looking upward at him.

Moreover, by showing us repeated scenes of his characters watching the monster's actions, Honda skillfully exploits subject–object correlation to make his audience feel invested in the unreality-as-reality of the events he depicts. Watching Yamane, Ogata, Emiko, or Shinkichi silently watching Gojira from the Shinagawa hill or dockside with expressions of grim resignation, viewers share their own spectatorship with the subjects in the film. Terry Morse recognizes and extends this technique in *Godzilla, King of the Monsters* as Steve Martin and Tomo Iwanaga cower literally below Godzilla's face on Hachiman Hill, channeling the shock and horror the sudden close up revelation of the creature is meant to convey to the audience.

Subsequently, as Martin watches and narrates Godzilla's rampage from his window in the Tokyo news office, American director Terry Morse focuses on his face, tense and sweating. Again, viewers of the monster's destruction of Tokyo are drawn into identification with Martin as subject. Finally, when Godzilla suddenly looms over an apartment building directly across the street, shot from below as though our beast

IX. The Science Fiction Rhetoric of Gojira

is towering above the audience as well, Martin gazes upward with practically the same combination of surprise and horror he exhibited on the path up Hachiman Hill. The monster's destiny has symbolically come full circle, and it implicates the audience's destiny as well.

There is more, however: this climactic moment effectively duplicates a scene from a few minutes earlier when Gojira incinerates a police car, including its occupants. In that scene the beast appears above an apartment block whose unsuspecting residents can be observed approaching their windows as if to see what's shaking their building and making all that noise. Then Godzilla focuses his atomic aerosol at the police car and, in another deft example of subject-object identification, the spectators of both film and carnage—the audience and the apartment dwellers—are gazing downward at the massacre of the policemen. As audience, even though we won't see the creature destroy that apartment, we know he is about to smash his way through the building and that those residents, who can't see him yet, are doomed. When Martin looks up and sees Godzilla appear over the adjacent rooftops, then push his way through the building which crumbles before him, we experience in retrospect what befell that residential block in the earlier scene.*

In fact Honda challenges the impossibility of there being a Gojira through the film's multiple layers of reference to Japanese drama, mythology, and recent history, but most of all, by having the monster tread a route through Tokyo most of which can still be followed today.† That route is demarcated by the destruction of actual Tokyo landmarks like the Shinagawa rail terminal, the Wako Department Store clock tower, the Toho Studios' own Nichigeki Theater, the Diet building, or the Kachidoki bridge. Constant intrusions into the film's fictional Japan, these veritable locations render Gojira's *non*existence problematic.

---

* This scene is duplicated in Shin Godzilla, but from the inside, when the larval Gojira topples an apartment building and we see a family inside being pitched towards the window as their home falls over.

† Gojira walks across the Sukiyabashi (bridge) towards Tokyo's Ginza district, forcing it to sink into the Ginza canal. Honda and Murata were clever about this because, as discussed in the Dramatis Personae chapter above, the bridge was the locus of *Kimi No Na Wa* (*What is your name?*), one of the first popular postwar radio soap operas. The bridge was subsequently torn down in 1957 to facilitate the construction of a subway line. During our tracing of the monster's route, we had to navigate around it.

In Search of Godzilla

The Question of Canonicity

"The question of the canon is one of the liveliest and most hotly debated in literary studies today, and the—at best—marginal position that science fiction occupies with regard to the most widely influential canons of literary value makes explicit consideration of canon-formation urgent," notes Freedman (24). If this is true of literary science fiction, how universally does it apply to cinema? The question is especially pertinent to *Gojira* as a science fiction film because it is no longer the curio or marginal cinematic text it was regarded as, when it was released in 1954. In part, this is because a sufficient number of other films in its sub-genres, the kaiju film and the radioactive mutation film, have since arrived to allow for comparative evaluations.

Also, the hands on the so-called "doomsday clock" have during the past three decades shifted further from midnight and then back towards it again. These fluctuations in the ethos have in turn shifted critical sensibilities from grave to relaxed or bemused and back to grave. This is all by way of saying the stature of *Gojira* and its various iterations have benefited from a variety of critical viewpoints and assessments. The stubbornness with which this film has remained in the discussion is hardly the least of its claims to canonicity.

To put it bluntly we, as critical viewers, have re-created *Gojira* (the film) no fewer times than Toho and the Monsterverse series have re-created the beast himself in the seventy years since its release in Nagoya. This assumes that the speculation of a film is an aesthetic act of reformulation. A viewer, creatively interacting with a film, is not passive. He or she becomes, in effect, a co-creator along with the cinematic text.

As Freedman notes, the future oriented genre of science fiction is typically at home in the most metropolitan regions of the most advanced nations (50). Japan quickly found itself rejoining that community after its misdirected attempts at hegemonism sent it crashing out of membership in 1945. Gojira is science fiction in Tokyo, but myth and fantasy on Odo Island. Moreover, Kyohei Yamani stands in the same relation to the science fictional creature as old Izuma does to the mythic; both tell the story of a revenant from an ancient world, one in terms of relict ritualism and the other in terms of scientific rationalism.

IX. The Science Fiction Rhetoric of Gojira

Yes, there is an implied evolution going on here. The monster's progress from myth and fantasy to historical development—i.e., from yokai to kaiju—is also a metaphor for Japan's attempted evolution from mystified bushido militarism to a bourgeois, commercial civilization. Hence we find him rising from the sea even as Japan became more progressively committed to the rule of commerce but the warrior ethos, in the form of the Castle Bravo test, threatened to drag it backwards towards its violent and hegemonic past.

The Hungarian critic Georg Lukács famously declared the novel the preeminent expression of emerging bourgeois civilization. In this sense, as well as for its cinematic heteroglossia, in which the clashing voices of the Japans of the antique and recent past and the complex present circle each other and collide, Lukács clearly fell short of anticipating how cinema would not only assume that role as well, but in terms of mass appeal effectively co-opt it in a post-textual world. Nonetheless, *Gojira* is also novelistic. It is an omnibus of features of a Japan reaching unabashedly beyond its sordid recent history for a civilized status bourgeois in its contemporaneous sense.

It is also an historical document, in terms both of its content and its stature. In its representation of Japanese civilization a decade removed from the Pacific War yet haunted, still, by that conflict, *Gojira* as science fiction is also an evolution of historical fiction. It was crucial to Honda his story be experienced as a serious critique of the history of violence. As Freedman put it, "The historical novel, then, is, to use the term that the philosophically erudite Lukács himself repeatedly employs with full intent, an eminently critical form, a form that constructs societies as radically historicized and complexly determined totalities" (44).

So then why did the Japanese film industry take so long to produce a major work of science fiction compared to the west? Part of the answer is that the Empire achieved modernity in Western terms quite late, in fits and starts from the moment Commodore Perry barged in and forced its hand:

> It may be that the futuristic orientation of science fiction requires a lengthier, more difficult gestation period, a more prolonged exposure to the ever more intense effects of technical and cultural modernity. Or, in somewhat different terms, the dramatization of the historicity of the present in relation to the future may be a more difficult critical operation than the comparable dramatization in relation to the past [Freedman 50].

In Search of Godzilla

Gojira, viewed from this perspective, is a *critical* work. The warning which underlies it meets the light of sunset in Yamane's comments, just after the monster dies, that there may be another Gojira in the world's future if nuclear testing continues. The paleontologist's realization that Gojira could not be the only one of his species infers that he must have parents if not siblings, and that very parentage all but guarantees, in Yamane's mind, the eventuality of another Gojira. Nevertheless, the *uber*-kaiju's revisitation does not merely symbolize the immanence of Japan's recent martial history. Japan's culture openly prides itself on its roots in antiquity, and as we have noted above, the film and its monster appear as part of the same cinematic ethos that gave us *The Seven Samurai* and a renaissance of bushido narratives. As Yamane's lecture to the Diet committee, complete with its geologic charts, plainly demonstrates, the creature drags along with it a much deeper antiquity. It is further ironic that a work so firmly connected to Japan's failure to outdistance both history and prehistory should turn so resolutely away from both.

X

Shin Gojira

Parody, Politics and Commentary

I'M GOING TO CONCLUDE MY DISCUSSION about the original *Gojira* with a look at two films which were both commentaries on, tributes to, and parodies of their 1954 predecessor.

Sixty-two years and nearly thirty sequels later Toho Studios reanimated its slumbering Godzilla franchise with *Shin Gojira*, which the studio described not as a sequel but as a "reboot." This term fuddles some kaiju fans. Briefly, it means the world of the new film inhabits a different dystopia from the older ones. Or, perhaps, that the monsters may change but the awe that conditions our confrontations with them does not. There never before had been anything like this Gojira who rose from Sagami Bay, even though that new cinematic reality is haunted by the old.

Toho's 2016 project was stimulated in no small part by the box office success of the Legendary Pictures American "monsterverse" Godzilla movies. Featuring a bulked-up, Ralph Kramden–like version of the monster (which must have ponged sumo in its Japanese releases), the Monsterverse gestures in its own, albeit superficial, way toward the Japanese original. Among its legacy acknowledgments it appropriated the name Dr. Serizawa and a few memes from the olden Toho series. These included the obligatory, and frankly by now tiresome, knockdown-dragout matches between Godzilla and other monsters, some of whom, like Megalon—a cross between a giant roach and Edward Scissorhands—look just plain silly.

As its predecessor had woven together many social, cultural, political and human strands, so does the reboot, with the added complexity of folding into itself much of the substance of Honda's masterpiece. Considered together, the two films are like a set of interlocking echo chambers. The new film emulates the creation of the original, as its two directors, Hideaki Anno and Shinji Higuchi, assumed many of the production roles of Ishiro Honda and Eiji Tsuburaya. Anno, a veteran of animated films including the genre-bending *Neon Genesis Evangelion*, was primarily in charge of its stunning special effects. The creature was brought to life through motion capture technology which, however much more advanced, still involved a human actor in a cybernetic outfit supplying its movements. Higuchi was also a veteran of *tokusatsu* films as various as *Gamera, Guardian of the Universe, Japan Sinks*, and *Attack on Titan*.

Shin Gojira hugs the contours of the original film and uses it extensively for background and ironic resonance. It redeploys snatches of Akira Ifukbe's 1954 score, woven through an intense new score by Shirō Sagisu. In another salute, it brings back the fictional Odo Island like some latter-day Brigadoon, as the birthplace of the mysterious Professor Goro Maki (whether his surname, suggesting a sushi roll, is meant to be funny or not I'll leave to the viewer) who named the creature Gojira after the island's legendry *kami*. His apparent suicide by drowning in Tokyo Bay opens the narrative where Daisuke Serizawa's self-immolation concluded the original.

Goro Maki is a composite figuration of several characters from the 1954 movie. Like *Gojira*'s Dr. Yamane he is a graying eminence whose knowledge about this new creature broods over the narrative. At the same time, Maki exhibits Serizawa's reluctance to share his research, leaving behind an all but indecipherable—and incomplete—genetic diagram of the creature. The senior biologist on the irreverent bureaucrat Rando Yaguchi's emergency team, Professor Hazama, operates on Maki's wavelength insofar as he understands the documents about the monster's metabolism and genetic makeup the mysterious academic left behind. Most important, Hazama realizes the significance of the origami figure discovered in Maki's boat. Before drowning himself, Maki leaves an *orizuru*, a folded paper crane, sitting atop a packet containing his complex diagram. The name of his boat, the *Glory Maru*. was also the name of the first ship sunk by the original Gojira. The paper crane is a cypher, a clue to how to read the diagram by folding it like an orizuru. As an opening salvo of nuclear disaster linked metaphors, the crane also evokes post–Hiroshima leukemia victim Sadako Sasaki's failed attempt to save herself by making a *senbazuro* of a thousand paper cranes.

X. Shin Gojira: *Parody, Politics and Commentary*

Other hark backs include the mauling of a JSDF tank brigade at close range, recalling the fate of the hapless 49th Armored Division which had tried to take the monster on at point blank range in the original film. Like Honda's monster, this one may appear in daylight but its real affinity is for darkness. Anno and Higuchi's creature husbands its potent radioactive breath and particle-beam power until after dark, until injured by a JDAM weapon, much as Gojira 54 forbore unleashing his toxic expectorant until electrocuted and bombarded. *Shin Gojira*'s most spectacular scene is the monster's counterattack, which the directors set up brilliantly by staging a citywide power failure just before the bombers strike. Gojira's atomic glow and fiery rage are all the more striking for the way they light up a darkened Tokyo at the moment of it destruction.

Perhaps worst of all, Japan's self-defense options are usurped by the United Nations, which plans by fiat to strike the monster with a nuclear warhead after giving the country two weeks to evacuate Tokyo and promising to rebuild it afterwards. This returns Japan to the dependent status in which it found itself during the Allied Occupation at the end of the Pacific War. As Yaguchi bitterly remarks to Cabinet Secretary Akasaka, "we're postwar dependents again, and postwar lasts forever." After Yaguchi's *Yoshiori* coagulant freezes Gojira and saves the city from nuclear annihilation, the creature stands frozen in front of the main Tokyo railroad station like a gigantic statue. It hilariously occupies the same spot where for decades a three meter high statue of Gojira '54 stood on its marble pedestal. Now, though, that older statue has been moved to the Toho Studios lobby and replaced with a somewhat larger figure of Shin Gojira.

Remaking Gojira

Anno and Higuchi take the malleability of the shapeshifting 1954 kaiju to new extremes, reconfiguring the creature in multiple distinctive forms. Through a series of stages it evolves, eventually, into a fully exfoliated monstrosity in all its Brobdingnagian essentials. As a simulacrum of its predecessor, Shin carries its withered hands held up and out, recalling the posture of *hibakusha*. Moreover, that *hibakusha*-like keloid scarring has metastasized to engulf and transform Gojira's entire physiognomy. Glowing with radioactivity through its semi-transparent torso, *Shin* is a specter composited of deformities, a barely saurian zombie. In *Gojira* destruction of the body is destruction of the whole body, not by dismemberment. In *Shin Gojra*, the creature is effectively turned inside out; we are teased by inferences of a backlit anatomy we aren't permitted to see until the enigmatic conclusion, when the beast attempts to regenerate in skeletonized, humanoid shapes.

Among the monster's few discernibly reptilian features is its expandable lower jaw, which widens like that of an African egg-eating snake (*Dasypeltis scabra*) to permit unobstructed projection of its updated version of the original's radioactive aerosol breath, modernized as a particle beam weapon.

If Goro Maki's name fan dances around some comic possibilities, so do the Yaguchi team's discussions of whether their Gojira can be killed or not, considering how many times the original had been dispatched in prior movies only to rise from the water again in the next one. Even though it is not a surviving prehistoric life form but a contemporaneous mutation of an unnamed sea creature whose ontogeny apparently recapitulates its phylogeny, you could imagine while beholding it that Gojira's H-bomb induced radiation sickness had progressed beyond scarring to full-blown teratogenicity. The original Gojira has evolved cinematically into a specter so ravaged it has become almost unbearable to behold, like a walking corpse. The team of scientists and renegade bureaucrats tasked with its destruction openly ponder whether it is even a living thing in any conventional sense. At times they seem to be discussing a gigantic virus or some immortal visitation.

Shin Gojira's ontic status is far more problematic than the original Gojira's, whom Dr. Yamane described as a survivor of both the Jurassic or Cretaceous eras and of the hydrogen bomb. He was not a reanimated corpse; he was not brought back from a non-living or dormant state. But Shin Gojira is represented as at least in a visual sense reanimated or, to invoke that classic horror movie sobriquet, undead. Dr. Yamane had argued that the monster should be studied and the Yaguchi team certainly pick up his dropped gantlet. They configure its molecular structure in charts, equations and computer graphics like any inorganic entity, while its corporeality is subverted by its ravaged appearance, its inside-out skeletal structure, and the chunks of meat that get blasted off of it. Its inner glow is caused by a nuclear life-support system, not even a

X. Shin Gojira: *Parody, Politics and Commentary*

metabolism such as living creatures possess,* which sustains its bodily presence.

This Gojira is plainly meant to disgust as well as horrify. As Aldana Reyes has noted,

> besides acting as the catalyst for the type of more instinctive reactions connected to the vicarious experience of imagined pain, the body can be a source of affect at a representational level when it dares to transgress the neatly delineated boundaries of inside and outside [29].

Viewers of monster movies expect to be shocked and disturbed. The *frisson* of that shock is what draws so many of them to the cinema in the first place.

It also appears to be in a state of decay; parts of it fall away as it expels gouts of blood-like fluids. The half reptilian, half humanoid creatures erupting from its tail, their own skeletons visible, are also walking dead. I earlier pointed out that the gendering of Gojira as male was a social and not a biological determination but in fact we don't really know its gender. Shin Godzilla both solves and muddles that conundrum. Could it be a parthenogen? There is also an element of horror in this final identification of the creature as mother, frozen in its parthenogenic attempt to expel its own death as progeny. That combined deadness and humanness, simultaneously, draw the viewer into an abject sense of identification with both. This, too, is resonant of Fukushima and its deadening of the once populated area around it, and the lingering threat of contamination and sickness it portends.

Both films are what Fukushima crisis historian Deirdre Langeland has called "disaster memories," in the sense that collective recall of catastrophes like wars, seismic events, or typhoons, migrate from acute personal recollections into historical documentation and eventually folklore. The cinematic scaffolding of *Shin Gojira* as disaster memory is the 1954 *Gojira* which was itself a composite disaster memory of the Pacific War, the atomic bombings, and the Castle Bravo contamination of the Lucky Dragon Five. The two films are concentric memorials. "But disaster memory isn't perfect," writes Langeland about Japan's long history of earthquakes and their attendant tsunamis. "Over time, it fades. As decades pass without a major disaster, people begin to move back

---

*The odd, sulfur-based metabolism of deep ocean volcanic vent coelenterates notwithstanding.

into the low-lying areas by the water" (131). We can see this dynamic operating both within and between both films.

Yoshikuni Igarashi referred to "markers of loss" as mnemonic aids fixing the terrors and damage of war in cultural consciousness, keeping disaster memory vivid and counteracting its tendency to fade. In *Shin Gojira* Assistant Cabinet Secretary Rando Yaguchi, nominally the protagonist of the film, resurrects such a marker when in response to bureaucratic overconfidence about eradicating the monster he specifically blames the hauteur of Showa-era Japanese militarism for the Pacific War deaths of three million Japanese. At the same time, a German supercomputing corporation is helpful in cracking the code of Goro Maki's diagram, redeeming the ugly background radiation of Serizawa's possible collaboration with Axis Germany. There does seem to be a self-conscious process of expiation at work here, best discerned by comparing both films.

Channeling the Fukushima Daiichi Disaster

Despite its enthusiastic reception in Japan, this winner of Best Picture at the Japan Film Awards seemed opaque in many ways to western audiences. Much of its very funny, if acerbic, critique of Japanese politics was unfortunately lost on American viewers and critics, who felt the film was "talky" and much of its content was somehow irrelevant to the spectacle of the monster itself. We can circumvent much of that opacity by turning our attention to the tragedy which resurrected Gojira from his twelve-year cinematic slumber.

Returning to the issue of disaster memory, lurking behind this new Gojira, as nuclear war and bomb tests lurked behind its predecessor, was a combined natural cataclysm and man-fangled catastrophe that still haunted Japan when the film was made. March hasn't been a lucky month in recent Japanese history. On March 1, 1954, the fishing boat Lucky Dragon Five was contaminated by the American hydrogen bomb test in the Marshall Islands. Three days later, as yet unaware of the fate of the boat and its crew, the Diet approved an ambitious program to nuclearize the national power grid. This eventually led to the construction of the massive Fukushima Daiichi six-reactor power plant (Lochbaum et al.: 40). With a particularly noxious irony, Fukushima Daiichi

X. Shin Gojira: *Parody, Politics and Commentary*

was constructed on the site of Iwaki Airfield, where kamikaze pilots trained (Kadota 119–123).

On March 11, 2011, the most powerful earthquake ever recorded in Japan—a brutal 9.1 on the Richter scale—struck the northeast coast of Honshu. In this megathrust type quake, the Pacific seafloor lurched beneath the western arm of the North American tectonic plate upon which northern Honshu and Hokkaido ride, yanking the continental plate downward and lowering the entire Sendai plain. This suppression of the coastline enabled the fifty-meter-high tsunami which followed to rush farther inland, swamping villages, cities, and public works. The wave swept thousands of victims out to sea as it receded. Even so, the most catastrophic consequences of the disaster unfolded over the next four days. The tsunami overtopped the protective sea walls around the Fukushima-Daiichi nuclear power station in coastal Ōkuma, causing the plant's auxiliary generators to fail and knocking out the coolant pumps to all six of its reactors.

Between March 12 and 14 three reactor cores melted down and the accumulated hydrogen gas within their containment buildings exploded, releasing lethal dosages of radiation into the atmosphere and sea. Many thousands of Japanese who had survived the quake and tidal wave now had to flee the region. It was Japan's worst atomic disaster since the bombings of its cities more than seven decades earlier. Over a period of several days, while the plant's operators struggled to bring the crisis under control, matters only grew worse.* The stages of Shin Gojira's evolution into ever bigger, more violent, and more destructive forms can be mapped over the worsening crisis at the plant. Three of its four forms were given names roughly corresponding to the areas of the city where they did the most damage. There's a delicious element of extended parody in those names, because they were marketing afterthoughts to designate the toy figurine versions of the creature. They are never mentioned in the film itself but they have found common usage in discussions about it.

Of its first unnamed aquatic form we only ever see its tail. Its *aji*-eyed larval form, wriggling destructively up the Nomi-gawa, has

---

* The film *Fukushima 50* (Kadokawa Daiei, 2020), starring Ken Watanabe—who also plays the reconstituted Dr. Serizawa in the American "monsterverse" Godzilla movies—as beleaguered plant manager Masao Yoshida, is a riveting account of the nuclear power plant crisis.

In Search of Godzilla

been dubbed *Kamata-kun*. The first erect—shall we call it pupal—form is *Shinegawa-kun* following its short but obligatory rampage through the same rail yard area first traversed by the original monster. And as the viewer—ever alert—doubtless realizes, the framing of its approach to a Shinegawa rail bridge resembles a scene from the original film. Its fourth and most awe-inspiring, fully developed, luminescent radioactive form is *Kamakura-san*, a comically honorific title akin to Mr. Gojira or Gojira, Sir. In this stage the creature has, so to speak, arrived like the plant onto the cusp of meltdown. In its counterattack against the military units assailing it, it discharges radioactivity in a barely controlled tantrum, inflecting the worst condition of the nuclear plant for which it is an extended metaphor.

Even the fate of the monster, frozen in place yet still radioactive and a threat to come back to life, is comparable to the condition of the plant. Both are "scrammed," as biologist Hiromi Ogashira puts it—shut down but not quite dead. Like the plant, useless, contaminated, and set off in its vast exclusion zone, Japan will have to live with the beast in its enforced dormancy. In its way the film's conclusion is also a confession of the permanence of geopolitical anxiety. As Nathaniel J. Dominy and Ryan Calsbeek have written,

> we suggest that Godzilla is evolving in response to a spike in humanity's collective anxiety. Whether reacting to geopolitical instability, a perceived threat from terrorists, or simply fear of "the other," many democracies are electing nationalist leaders, strengthening borders, and bolstering their military presence around the world.

Fukushima contributed to that anxiety by providing a glimpse of just how destructive a nuclear reactor meltdown could be.

Paralyzed by indecision, incompetence, and inexperience, the Japanese government, the Tokyo electric utility TEPCO which owned the plant, and various bureaucratic agencies charged with promulgating and enforcing safety standards fumbled their responses to the Fukushima-Daiichi crisis in a black comedy of errors. Lochbaum paints a picture of a fiasco in progress:

> Tapes from the videoconference link between the Seismic Isolation Building and TEPCO headquarters, released by TEPCO more than a year later, reveal a chaotic scene. ... Tempers flare as Yoshida and his team are besieged with orders and counterorders from TEPCO headquarters, which was also getting instructions from the prime minister's office [87].

X. Shin Gojira: *Parody, Politics and Commentary*

The movie's repeated scenes of frustrated officials and bureaucrats marching up and down the halls of the Prime Minister's office building, from one truncated conference to another, reflects the confusion and indecision that reigned at the highest echelons of government.

Journalist Ryūshō Kadota interviewed Masao Yoshida months after he left TEPCO to deal with medical issues:

> Prime minister [Naoto] Kan insisted on visiting the site in person, which only distracted Yoshida and his crew from the critical work they had to do to keep the reactors under some semblance of control. "Kan could contribute nothing to the situation, and the plant could not spare a radiation suit or mask for him. He didn't deliberately make a nuisance of himself. It was just plain ignorance on his part. From that point of view, I wish the experts had told him more beforehand" [97].

Widely criticized for his handling of the situation, Prime Minister Kan resigned in its wake. Anno and Higuchi were less forgiving to his cinematic simulacrum, Prime Minister Seiji Okochi, who dies with most of his cabinet when their helicopter is struck by Gojira's particle beam.

The details of how the disaster unfolded and the government's efforts to deal with it have been extensively documented and retold so there's no need to go into it in detail here. Less well known is the backstory of the young seismologist Katsuhiko Ishibashi. In 1976 he proposed his theory of *genpatsu-shinsai*, that a quake-induced complete failure of a nuclear power station was entirely possible. His ideas that a seismic event "beyond design basis," in the benign parlance of pro-nuclear engineers and politicians, could occur, were largely ignored. He was removed from the official commission charged with establishing guidelines for plant safety (Lochbaum 40–42). Ishibashi is a partial model for *Shin Gojira*'s outspoken junior cabinet secretary Rando Yaguchi.

Tandem directors Anno and Higuchi drew heavily and in detail from the Fukushima Daiichi disaster for their creative recapitulation of what happened on March 3, 2011. "Anyone working in an area where radioactive materials may have been is required to wear a radiation suit—usually coveralls that are fastened tightly at the ankles and wrists, gloves, special socks, boots, goggles, and a breathing mask with a filter," relates Langeland (100). Yaguchi's coagulant crew wears identical garb. In a sense, cooling Gojira is like redemption for the failure to cool those reactors. "Make him scram [shut himself down] to save himself," Hiromi Ogashira says.

Indeed. The Great East Japan Earthquake, tsunami, and power plant meltdowns engendered *Shin Gojira* much as Hiroshima, Castle Bravo, the Myōjin Shō eruption, and the Lucky Dragon incident collectively birthed *Gojira*. Yet 12 years earlier, there had been another nuclear plant crisis which should have been taken as a warning of what might come. The Tokaimura crisis, at the country's very first nuclear power station, prefigured Fukushima when enriched fuel for an experimental fast breeder reactor went critical (Lochbaum 38–39). It was barely contained. Nobody in authority seemed to have learned much from it.

American advisors dispatched from Washington and from the Nuclear Regulatory Commission to assist their Japanese colleagues were appalled by the confusion and bureaucratic infighting they encountered. They found themselves repeatedly at loggerheads with their hosts. "For a moment, the magnitude of the crisis for the Japanese overwhelmed [U.S. engineer] Casto, who noted that a thousand bodies had washed ashore from the tsunami." Yet appreciating the severity of the problem, the Americans were not entirely unsympathetic. "'[I]t's hell over here for that government. I mean, it's just absolutely hell. And I know we get frustrated with them, but, man, when you think about what they're faced with, it's absolutely unfathomable'" (Lochbaum 99).

Even so, the United States, much to the displeasure of the Japanese government, acted on the advice of its own experts on the scene and began advising American civilian residents and military personnel to evacuate a much wider area in northern and eastern Honshu than the Kan administration wished. The Japanese officials were fearful that if the public heard about this warning, it would cause wider panic. In *Shin Gojira*, while officials debate whether Gojira is radioactive enough to represent a threat, an unnamed U.S. aircraft carrier makes an unscheduled departure from Yokosuka naval station because it has detected radiation emitted by the monster. Even this vignette has its basis in history. Following the quake and tsunami the aircraft carrier USS *Ronald Reagan* was stationed off Sendai with food, equipment and medical supplies for the stricken region. However, when the ship detected the irradiated water pouring from the plant and found itself in a pool of contamination, it was forced to withdraw to 200 miles out to sea (Langland 97).

X. Shin Gojira: *Parody, Politics and Commentary*

Such episodes do remind us that Gojira's radioactivity is essential to his charisma, a foundation of his personality, as it were.

In their haste to keep the failing reactor cores cool, Yoshida and his crew, their freshwater cooling tanks exhausted, had to pump seawater into the containment buildings but that water, now irradiated, flowed back into the plant's discharge canal, which normally carried heated water from the plant to the ocean. The water was contaminated with cobalt, cesium-137, and iodine. Lochbaum tells us,

> Before the disaster, the waters off Fukushima Prefecture had supported a thriving commercial fishing industry. The tsunami had wreaked havoc on its fleets, ports, and processing facilities. The prospect that seafood taken from these waters might now be contaminated and unsafe to eat threatened to deliver another blow to the devastated region [156–157].

The irradiation of its offshore fisheries invoked once again the contamination which followed the Cattle Bravo test and the distribution of the Lucky Dragon's catch in 1954 before anyone understood what had happened to it.

Fukushima made Japan look vulnerable, conclusively popping the bubble of the already declining Japanese economic juggernaut. In that sense, *Shin Gojira* is a starting over not just in terms of the beast itself, or even of his cinematic franchise, but of the Japan he inhabits—a Japan which, after the Fukushima catastrophe, looked naked without him. Japan needed Gojira back, if only because his jagged back was powerful enough to bear such a freight of metaphor. Michael J. Blouin wrote perspicaciously, a few years before Toho greenlighted the new film,

> Even when discourse surrounding nuclear issues falls into hushed whispers, the giant lizard will not be ignored. And although undoubtedly the remains from Japan's recent disaster will cede to political posturing, I presume that Godzilla will not exit quietly from the stage with tail between legs [100].

The Political Parody

Shin Gojira "introduces everyone with on-screen text," writes Harrison Chute, "as if daring us to play detective matching the fictional character's title to their real-world counterpart in March 2011." Such a heuristic exercise would doubtless be easier for Japanese who remember the twisted comedy of obfuscation that played out over national television during the time of the disaster. For the rest of us, Chute has provided a list of the notable figures involved in miscommunicating to the public, conveniently matched with their doppelgängers in the film, on the East Asian interest web magazine *Eyes East*. I invite our readers to note the article's URL in the reference section below.

In true Japanese fashion, we are granted an aerial view of raucous nighttime street rallies taking the monster's side in its confrontation with the authorities. Yaguchi and his team, sequestered several stories above them in the Prime Minister's residence, sleep through the noise. Some bureaucratic habits are tough to shake. The demonstrations in *Shin Gojira* are not only parodies of Kyohei Yamane's solicitude for Gojira in the original. They also satirize the huge anti-nuclear demonstrations following Fukushima. Those rallies grew in size and anger with each new revelation about what their government had kept from them and how badly their responses had been screwed up. The demonstrators in the film, chanting "Gojira is God. Save Gojira!" inadvertently *support* the radioactive threat. That's a commentary on how political passions cloud logic, and it's also pretty funny.

There are quite a few comic moments in *Shin Gojira* aside from that one. One of the funniest sequences in the film features an early meeting between Prime Minister Okochi and a trio of middle-aged biology experts who demur and refuse to offer explanations of the creature for fear of damaging their reputations. Meanwhile, the Prime Minister sits impatiently thrumming his fingers. In another scene, the ominous music accompanying Gojira's ponderous advance out of Sagami Bay overlaps Okochi's entrance into the main conference room, drawing an ironic comparison between them.

Rando Yaguchi is backhandedly rewarded for his outspokenness by being assigned to head a team of misfits to study and recommend responses to the creature. Each time he reappears onscreen his name is preceded by an ever-lengthening list of titles and duties. Eventually he pulls together his band of "people with balls," a group one of his lieutenants, Health Policy Bureau Chief Mori, describes as "a crack team of lone wolves, nerds, troublemakers, outcasts, academic heretics and general pains in the bureaucracy," to circumvent the bumbling politicians and self-interested corporate nabobs who are making a hash of the crisis.

X. Shin Gojira: *Parody, Politics and Commentary*

In addition to nonconforming geologist Katsuhiko Ishibashi, Yaguchi most closely resembles Masao Yoshida, the plant manager at Fukushima Daiichi. As the danger of a meltdown increased, Yoshida advised his superiors he was going to pump seawater into the plant. Officials at TEPCO, worried about corrosion of their expensive equipment, dragged their feet on the decision. In one of the defining acts of heroic defiance which characterized Yoshida's stewardship of the crisis, he ignored a direct order from his superiors at TEPCO to postpone the injection of seawater and arranged for it to begin anyway (Lochbaum 62). Subsequently, though, as that seawater leached back into the plant's drainage system, it released Cesium 137 and other dangerous isotopes into the ocean for months. Our new Shin Gojira, remember, was mutated by his exposure to just such radioactive waste dumped into the sea.

The Pressure Pump Idea

The telescoping pressure booms used to inject Gojira with coagulant, called *kirin* or giraffes, also derive from the plant disaster. The method was close at hand because it had been proposed for Fukushima. These pumping vehicles were needed to replace the failed coolant systems at the reactor buildings, as Lochbaum notes:

> Fortunately, Unit 3 had an emergency cooling system that was still functional: the "high-pressure coolant injection" system or HPCI (pronounced hip-sea). When water levels dropped in the core, the HPCI automatically kicked in about an hour later, also drawing on battery power. Under normal circumstances, the RCIC was used to deliver makeup water to replace coolant boiled away by decay heat [66].

As the "Yaguchi Plan" begins rapidly to take shape, Defense Policy General Director Sodehara, a soldier who is part of the emergency council, presciently holds up a photo of a telescoping pressure pump as an ideal way to administer the "Yoshiori" coagulant to Gojira. Yaguchi names this coagulant solution after an episode from the *Nihon Shoki* wherein the trickster Susanoo intoxicates an eight-headed dragon menacing a divine princess before slaying it. Thus *Shin Gojira*, like its 1954 predecessor, defaults to Japanese mythology at one of its most crucial moments. A multi-layered reference, like so many in Anno and Higuchi's film, this solution also has precedent in the struggle to contain the damage at the Fukushima Daiichi nuclear plant. As the calamity spiraled out of control, engineers from the plant and TEPCO desperately sought assistance from foreign powers with the expertise and equipment to bring matters under control, especially ways to inject cooling water into the plant. Turning to the American technical experts who had been sent to assist their Japanese colleagues by the U.S. nuclear agency, "Two government ministry employees had asked for help acquiring emergency equipment ... [including] four or five trucks with aerial booms capable of spraying water at a height of sixty-five to one hundred feet (twenty to thirty meters) to reach the fuel pools" (Lochbaum 91).

The trucks, equipped with booms capable of extending about 200 feet, could remotely spray seawater into the fuel pools with precision. Two such trucks were in Japan, and additional ones could be obtained from abroad (Lochbaum 101). The pumping vehicles and tanker trucks used to store the Yoshiori coagulant, like those requisitioned for the nuclear plant, are obtained from China in the film. So, if military attaché Sodehara seemed to have the pumping crane idea and photos so conveniently at hand, it was simply a matter of having resorted to them before to bring the reactors under control.

XI

Another Postscript
Godzilla Minus One

The most recent iteration of Toho's Godzilla series is *Godzilla Minus One* (*Gojira mainasu wan*, 2023) which, like *Shin Godzilla* before it, deserves some serious discussion. *Minus One* is both a tribute to, and a sophisticated commentary upon, the original *Gojira*. It treats the 1954 film and its titular monster as its foundational work, while at the same time presenting itself as a stand-alone feature. Perhaps more importantly, it revisits the crucial years between the end of the Pacific War and the beginnings of Japanese reconstruction. *Minus One* also delves into major themes and characters from the previous films of its award-winning auteur. The runup to and late stages of the Pacific War, the psychological struggles of reluctant soldiers, naval officers, and airmen, and the rebuilding period of Japan which followed, have been leitmotifs of Takashi Yamazaki's works since he began helming his movies.

Visible recapitulations of scenes from his *Always: Sunset on Third Street* triptych, *The Great War of Archimedes*, and above all his masterpiece *The Eternal Zero*, populate the Godzilla movie he has stated he always dreamed of making. The social fabric of Japan was being re-woven, establishing the economy and the culture which *Gojira* first engaged. After an extended run of releases from *Godzilla Raids Again* (1955) through *Final Wars* (2004) during which Godzilla had gradually become initially benign and even heroic, in both *Shin Godzilla* and *Minus One* the creature has become destructive again. Not coincidentally Russia, China, and the United States have become more hostile to one another, as though the kaiju genre has been following the hands of the doomsday clock towards midnight. Kōichi's nightmares also remind us that the creature is no less than civilization's bad dream of itself.

As in Ishiro Honda's cinematic vision, the influence of Akira

In Search of Godzilla

Kurosawa broods over Yamazaki's narratives and imagery, especially in his representations of immediate postwar Japan. The domestic saga of Kōichi and Noriko takes the form of a *shomin geki,* or bourgeois drama, imparting a sense of familiarity that contrasts with the movie's fantastic elements. Much of this film's pathos draws upon the late master's vision of early Occupation era economic struggle. We can readily discern the revenant Tokyo and its forlorn inhabitants of *One Wonderful Sunday, Stray Dog, Ikiru, Do-des-ka-den*—especially referenced by the Tokyo streetcars Godzilla sends flying—and even Kurosawa's late masterpiece, *Madadayo,* in which Yamazaki regular Hidetaka Yoshioka (the naval engineer Noda in *Godzilla Minus One*) made one of his earliest film appearances. Watching the scene of Noda, the minesweeper crew, and Kōichi's and Noriko's makeshift family enjoying tea and saki in their reconstructed home is, indeed, redolent of the recurrent *mada-hai* party *mis-en-scène* of *Madadayo.*

Yamazaki's *Always: Sunset* series also draws from Kurosawa's representations of the postwar period while simultaneously revealing the younger auteur's fascination with Gojira, who stars in an impressive cameo. The monster emerges into view from a barely recovering Tokyo now thrown into chaos, and briefly shakes himself off like a wet dog. That annoyed, distracted Gojira was a harbinger of the vengeful beast with which Yamazaki would present us in *Minus One.*

Godzilla Minus One revisits several themes which have been Godzilla standards since the 1954 original. Once again the creature is a product of nuclear radiation but this time its origin is more explicitly defined as a teratogenic version of a contemporary Lazarus taxon as well as a victim not of the Castle hydrogen bomb tests but of the Crossroads atomic bomb tests of the late 1940s. Filling in some missing details from the original film, *Minus One* reminds us that Gojira would have been subject to the Crossroads tests which preceded the fateful Castle series that takes center stage in the original film. Gojira, seen from this perspective, may well have been a product of all the nuclear tests to which the Marshall Islands were subjected, not just the thermonuclear blasts which followed.

Takashi Yamazaki already had a résumé of sophisticated anime as well as serious historical drama. His *The Great War of Archimedes* (2019) was a study in the corruption and delusional thinking that led Japan into the disaster of the Pacific War. Yamazaki symbolized the

XI. Another Postscript: Godzilla Minus One

hubris of that period in the form of the Imperial Japanese Navy's determination to build an impregnable battleship, the *Yamato*, even though more far-sighted officers like Admiral Isoroku Yamamoto already understood the growth of naval air power made such ships obsolete.

Yamazaki's earlier film, *The Eternal Zero* (2013, also released as *The Fighter Pilot*), is widely considered a classic war movie. It deals with the same themes of courage versus cowardice among kamikaze pilots, and the question of when suicidal loyalty becomes a mere waste of life, to which Yamazaki would return in *Godzilla Minus One.* For all his nuanced problems, failed kamikaze pilot Kōichi's guilt and shame are on the surface. Moreover, Kōichi is like a mirror image, a reversal, of Serizawa. His ultimate survival offsets Serizawa's suicide even though he is another tormented figure in the later film. Like the Odo Island Yamabushi Tengu ritual which succeeded maiden sacrifices to Gojira, Kōichi's narrow survival via ejector seat when he crashes his Shinden fighter into Godzilla's mouth is a symbolic stand-in for, or redemption of, the suicide he refused to commit as a kamikaze pilot. We have already discussed how Serizawa's anguish could have roots in his wartime work as well as in his moribund relations with Emiko, all of which are inflected in Kōichi's asexual relationship with Noriko. At the same time, his wartime cowardice mirrors Serizawa's guilt over his terrifying discovery.

Yamazaki introduces us to Godzilla as the pre-mutated, smaller, but still formidable saurian *yokai* of Odo Island near the beginning of the film. When it emerges to savage a Japanese airfield and slaughter its troops, we also learn the islanders have said it "brings up" deep sea fish whenever it appears. Odo's inhabitants clearly have a long familiarity with it, but also one which is more current than the ancient legend of Gojira in the original film. About a year after the attack on the airfield we actually see this creature, submerged, being irradiated by the first Crossroads atomic test at Bikini Atoll, and not liking it one bit. We also learn of a number of ship sinkings which follow its contamination and indicate the magnitude of its growth.

The frigate squad depth bombing of Gojira is amplified here into a pitched battle with the sole remaining armed IJN warship, the battle cruiser *Takao*. This is a memorable set piece. The fate of the *Takao*, a sitting duck for Godzilla's atomic breath, also evokes the disastrous last moments of the fabled battleship *Yamato* from Yamazaki's earlier film, *The Great War of Archimedes*.

In Search of Godzilla

Most amusing, perhaps, about this violent and uncompromising film is how closely it tracks the 1947 monster broadcast hoax, mentioned in Chapter 1 above, which was perpetrated by the U.S. Occupation radio station. Early on, *Minus One* gives us several date markers which conclude with the epic *Jaws*-inspired boat chase in "May 1947." We next find the injured Kōichi recuperating in a clinic and making his way back to his surrogate family, Noriko, and her adopted daughter Akiko. Perhaps we can be forgiven for identifying an early scene of Noriko cradling the orphaned Akiko with Emiko Yamane's comforting of an orphaned toddler in the charnel environment of a hospital in *Gojira*. This passage of a few weeks since the boat chase brings us to the appearance of Godzilla in Tokyo in June 1947, the same time as the hoax broadcast. Like the hoax, we first hear of a giant creature emerging from Tokyo Bay through the family's radio. Also as in the hoax, which featured background cannon fire, three war vintage Japanese tanks shell the creature to little effect. Moreover these tanks recall the unfortunate 49th Armored Division annihilated by Gojira in 1954.

Godzilla Minus One *as Alternative History*

Minus One is an alternative history not only to *Gojira*, but also to Japan's political situation depicted in its 1946–47 time frame. How alternative it is, is instructive about Yamazaki's narrative approach. In Yamazaki's 1947 General MacArthur bows out of dealing with the monster, citing his unwillingness to ruffle Stalin's feathers with large scale troop movements. This was a facile way to confine *Minus One*'s narrative to the efforts of the Japanese to defend themselves at a time when they had so little with which to do so. It is the one false note sounded by Yamazaki's screenplay. In fact, the fiercely conservative MacArthur was pugnacious and would not have shrunk from defending his troops from a threat like Godzilla, the delicate sensibilities of the Soviets notwithstanding. Stalin's forces had occupied all of the northernmost Japanese territory of Sakhalin and were openly eyeing Hokkaido, but the Supreme Commander assigned the U.S. 11th Airborne Division to Hokkaido to draw the line at the Sōya Strait.

In early 1947, the Japanese military had been demobilized and its new security services like the Coast Guard and Japan Defense Force

XI. Another Postscript: Godzilla Minus One

were still works on paper. This was a problem with which Honda did not have to contend; by 1954, the Coast Guard had been equipped with surplus frigates and destroyers, and the Defense Forces with surplus tanks, artillery, and aircraft. Meanwhile, there were more than 430,000 American troops and 40,000 British troops occupying Japan at the time of *Minus One*, with several hundred thousand of them stationed in the Tokyo–Yokohama axis alone. They are never shown in *Minus One*, so the tacit assumption is that MacArthur must have moved them to safety. In any case, the absence of direct American support suited both Honda's and Yamazaki's emphasis on Japanese self-reliance.

Likewise, the Japanese government demurs and will not take overt action to defend the country against this serious threat, leaving Noda and his colleagues, former naval officers and crews, to implement their own countermeasures. In fact, the government was in a state of transition in 1946–47. Emperor Hirohito had been reduced to a figurehead and the old Meiji constitution was being scrapped and rewritten under MacArthur's guidance as a democratic but also pacifistic document. Ergo, the inability of the government to respond effectively to Gojira makes a little more sense than the complete non-participation of allied occupation troops. During his assault on the Ginza district Godzilla is opposed by a handful of obsolete tanks, Type 3 Ho-Ni III self-propelled artillery vehicles, which seem to be all the government could get permission from the occupation to arm and use. Predictably, they're only effective enough to anger the monster and goad him into unleashing his atomic breath against the city.

The Japanese battle cruiser *Takao*, which saves Noda and his crew, was an historical ship so badly damaged by allied torpedo and bombing attacks in November 1944 that she was considered irreparable and moored at Singapore as an anti-aircraft platform. At the end of the war she suffered the ignominious fate of being sunk as a Royal Navy target ship. However, in *Minus One* she still has her big guns intact, though she winds up being sunk by Godzilla's atomic breath. Her disposition makes for an interesting contrast with Noda's flotilla, a couple of destroyers with their turrets stripped of their guns. It appears that, like the old tanks stationed in the Ginza, the cruiser was being held in reserve with the indulgence of the Occupation because they knew the monster was out there somewhere and these scrapheap armaments were expendable.

In Search of Godzilla

The one piece of military hardware which ultimately prevails against Godzilla is the warehoused J7W Shinden interceptor upon which the mechanic Tachibana, the only other survivor of Godzilla's attack on Odo Island, must exercise all his skills to make flyable for Kōichi to enact his symbolic kamikaze mission. There are a number of interesting aspects to the resurrection of this airplane. First of all, it was designed as a countermeasure to the American B-29 bomber. Japanese antiaircraft guns and even the vaunted A6M Zero could not reach the big plane, squadrons of which had been savaging Japanese cities, especially Tokyo, with near impunity. In this sense, the B-29 was an avatar of Godzilla himself.

Unfortunately for the Imperial Japanese military, the Shinden came too late in the war and with the country's industrial capabilities already devastated, it was never put into production. As carrier of the Hiroshima and Nagasaki atomic bombs, as well as the incendiary bombs which had reduced most of Tokyo to scorched rubble, the B-29 carries heavy negative symbolism for the Japanese, even today. That Kōichi should use an interceptor specifically designed against it to finish Godzilla off entails a redemptive *frisson*.

Given his anguish over his wartime failures, which he keeps hidden from Noriko until the reappearance of Godzilla forces him to reveal it, Kōichi occupies a dramatic function similar to Serizawa. The chemist had kept his secret fears about the oxygen destroyer from Emiko until the menace of Gojira occasioned Hagiwara's revelatory interview. Whereas Kōichi's heartbreak is personal and its causes are recent, Yamane and Serizawa are vessels of a more complicated despair. But like Kōichi, Yamane is also a victim of survivor's guilt. In his case he is the last member of the samurai class still standing. We know he is a relic of that class because he lives far too well for a college professor. Emiko is the symbol of his fleeting wealth, having thrown off the arranged marriage imposed on her by her parents and the parents of Dr. Serizawa.

Paleontology—the study of disappeared life—becomes, like Gojira himself, symbolic of loss on a colossal scale. Serizawa, too, as played by the veteran actor Akihiko Hirata (whose birth name, Akihiko Onoda, is honored by Yamazaki who calls the naval engineer proposing the freon weapon in *Minus One* Noda), is a relict samurai or most likely he would not have been the prospective groom in a family-arranged marriage, since betrothals were generally kept within similar social classes. The

XI. Another Postscript: Godzilla Minus One

eminent scientist, whose posh home and elaborately equipped laboratory also suggests either inherited wealth or prior government indulgence of his work, is somewhat younger than his would-be father in law but similarly carries within himself the darkness of the decline of his class. One can readily see it in his face, in the grimness of his moods and expressions. His oxygen destroyer, and the apparent German connection at the inference of which he bristles, like Yamane's paleontology ripples with grim backstories.

Both of these scientists share a terrible but subtle awareness of social decay and concomitant class decline they cannot redeem. Serizawa, with his suicide, finally does resolve his personal and cultural Gordian knots. Kōichi resolves his by symbolically reenacting the dutiful *kamikaze* suicide he had avoided. This symbolic enactment echoes the way the original film, as we noted multiple times above, ameliorated the literal human sacrifices of ancient tradition and recent valorization of glorious death alike. Tragically, though, Yamane is left walking alone across the deck of the Coast Guard vessel at the conclusion of *Gojira*, head bent down, shoulders slumped, crushed by his *anagnorisis* that other Gojiras were likely inevitable, and relegated to a background figure posed against a sunset.

Epilogue

It's an odd project, writing an epilogue to a saga that keeps unfolding and shows no sign of running out of radioactive steam. Godzilla continues to evolve, not just in the sense of the newer versions of the beast's metamorphoses—though there is that—but in the wider range of interpretations of him which have steadily become possible. Not the least of those were *Shin Gojira* and *Godzilla Minus One*. Contemplating the new films' wealth of inflections of characters, events and images from Honda's original brings into focus elements and relationships within the original film. Without these extended glosses, which is what these so-called "reboots" were, original elements of the 1954 groundbreaker would have been less than obvious. I hope we have illuminated much of that expansion of possible meanings here.

In the seven decades since Gojira first lurched out of Tokyo Bay, crashing our dreams and the worldwide cultural imagination, his legacy continues to grow. New Godzilla films, American and Japanese, are currently in production and there's no doubt others will follow them. New videos and podcasts about the world's most influential monster appear online every week. Professional as well as dilettante scholarship proliferate, the latter fueled by internet aficionados of kaiju films in general as well as of Godzilla in particular. You can bet this won't be the last critical study to find its way into print, either. There are also Japanese studies of Godzilla which have yet to be translated into English or other western languages. Tosio Takahasi's 1999 *At Night When Godzilla Comes* is a reputedly excellent study and meditation on the monster's history and significance to Japanese culture but, sadly, remains untranslated. Perhaps we'll see a reliable English translation eventually.

I hope that, if anything, I've made clear that *Gojira* is a product of a complicated civilization, conceived and created during an unfathomably complicated moment in its history. It asks, though not always

Epilogue

directly, difficult moral questions about our applications not only of technology but also of religious and artistic customs and traditions which remain material even now, seven decades later. They are questions that needed to be asked when it was made, and given the turbulence of history, they will doubtless still be worthy of asking into the unforeseeable future.

Miami, Florida
Halloween week, 2024

References

Aldana Reyes, Xavier. *Horror Film and Affect*. London: Routledge, 2016.
Allison, Anne. *Millennial Monsters: Japanese Toys and the Global Imagination*. Berkeley: University of California P, 2006.
Ancient worlds. [A website on ancient myths.] 2002–2013. Retrieved from http://www.ancientworlds.net/aw/Post/1261611.
Anderson, Joseph L. "Spoken Silents in the Japanese Cinema: Essay on the Necessity of Katsuben." *Journal of Film and Video* 40, no. 1 (Winter 1988): 13–33. https://www.jstor.org/stable/20687801. Retrieved 8/1/22.
Anderson, Mark. "Mobilizing *Gojira*: Mourning Modernity as Monstrosity," in William M. Tsutsui and Michiko Ito, eds., *In Godzilla's Footsteps: Japanese Pop Culture Icons on the Global Stage*. New York: Palgrave Macmillan, 2006. 21–40.
Andrews, Roy Chapman. *This Business of Exploring*. New York: G.P. Putnam, 1935.
Barr, Jason. *The Kaiju Film: A Critical Study of Cinema's Biggest Monsters*. Jefferson: McFarland, 2016.
Barthes, Roland. *Elements of Semiology*. Annette Lavers and Colin Smith, tr. New York: Hill and Wang, 1967.
_____. *Empire of Signs*. Richard Howard, tr. New York: Hill and Wang, 1982.
Blouin, M.J. *Japan and the Cosmopolitan Gothic: Specters of Modernity*. New York: Palgrave Macmillan, 2013.
Bogue, Mike. *Apocalypse Then: American and Japanese Atomic Cinema, 1951–1967*. Jefferson: McFarland, 1967.
Boss, J.E. "Hybridity and Negotiated Identity in Japanese Popular Culture," in W. Tsutsui and M. Ito, eds., *In Godzilla's Footsteps: Japanese Pop Culture Icons on the Global Stage*. New York: Palgrave Macmillan, 2006, 103–110.
Bradbury, Ray. "The Fog Horn," in *The Stories of Ray Bradbury*. New York: Rosetta Books, 1980, 266–272.
Brems, Brian. "Lost: Akira Kurosawa Noir." *Vague Visages*, January 18, 2021. https://vaguevisages.com/2021/01/18/lost-akira-kurosawa-noir/. Retrieved 07/24/2022.
The Broomcloset. Benten: Japanese Goddess of Eloquence. [Web log post.] March 8, 2013. http://broomcloset.wordpress.com/2013/03/08/benten-Japanese-goddess-of-eloquence/. Retrieved 6/4/22.
Brothers, Peter H. *Atomic Dreams and the Nuclear Nightmare: The Making of Godzilla (1954)*. Seattle: CreateSpace, 2015.
_____. *Mushroom Clouds and Mushroom Men: The Fantastic Cinema of Ishiro Honda*. Seattle: CreateSpace, 2013.
Burden, W. Douglas. *Dragon Lizards of Komodo: An Expedition to the Lost World of the Dutch East Indies*. New York: G.P. Putnam's Sons, 1927 (facsimile edition).

References

Campbell, Joseph. *Primitive Mythology: The Masks of God, Vol. 1.* New York: Viking, 1968.
Carrozza, J.L. *Japanese Special Effects Cinema: Godfathers of Tokusatsu, Vol. 1.* Tokyo: Orochi Books, 2022.
Charles River Editors. *The Axis Powers' Nuclear Weapons Program.* Cambridge, MA, 2015.
Chute, Harrison. "Your Guide to the Politics of *Shin Godzilla.*" *With Eyes East.* https://witheyeseast.com/2021/03/01/shin-godzilla-politics/#:~:text=Prime%20Minister%20Seiji%20Okouchi%20%2F%20Naoto%20Kan&text=As%20the%20head%20of%20state,character%20on%20the%20world%20stage. Retrieved 1/12/23.
Cortázar, Julio. *Literature Class: Berkeley 1980.* Katherine Silver, tr. New York: New Directions, 2013.
Dominy, Nathaniel J., and Ryan Carlsbeek, "A Movie Monster Evolves, Fed by Fear." *Science* #364 (May 2019): 840–841.
Dym, Jeffrey. "A Brief History of *Benshi* (Silent Film Narrators)." *Japan Society.* https://aboutjapan.japansociety.org/a_brief_history_of_benshi. Retrieved 7/30/22.
Ellwood, Robert S. "A Japanese Mythic Trickster Figure, Susa-no-o," in William Haynes and William Doty, eds., *Mythical Trickster Figures.* Tuscaloosa: U of Alabama P, 1993, 141–158.
Encyclopedia of Shinto. 2002–2006. Tokyo: Institute of Japanese Culture and Classics, Kokugakuin University. Retrieved from http://eos.kokugakuin.ac.jp/modules/xwords/entry.php?entryID=%20795.
Fay, Stephanie. "Why Godzilla Is Far Deeper Than You Think." Retrieved from https://web.archive.org/web/20150325090704/https://stephaniefay.hubpages.com/hub/Why-Godzilla-is-Far-Deeper-Than-You-Think.
Foster, Michael Dylan. *The Book of Yōkai: Mysterious Creatures of Japanese Folklore.* Oakland: U of California P, 2015.
_____. *Pandemonium and Parade: Japanese Monsters and the Culture of Yōkai.* Berkeley: U of California P, 2009.
Fradken, Lloyd. "Willis O'Brien, 1925's 'The Lost World' and the Story of Gwangi." http://www.bewaretheblog.com/2020/06/willis-obrien-1925s-lost-world-and.html. Retrieved 1/24/2023.
"Frank Iwanaga parting from a friend for work and school." Calisphere. https://calisphere.org/item/be4763518680ab5f8b673ed7055165d2/. Retrieved 8/6/22.
Freedman, Carl. *Critical Theory and Science Fiction.* Middletown: Wesleyan UP, 2000.
Galbraith, S. *The Emperor and the Wolf.* New York: Faber & Faber, 2002.
Galbraith, S., with F. Yukari and S. Atsushi. *Monsters Are Attacking Tokyo.* Los Angeles: Feral House, 1998.
Gerow, Aaron. "Wrestling with Godzilla: Intertextuality, Childish Spectatorship and the National Body." In Tsutsui and Ito, 63–81.
Gilmore, David D. *Monsters: Evil Beings, Mythical Beasts, and All Manner of Imaginary Terrors.* Philadelphia: U of Pennsylvania P, 2003.
Godzilla, the King of the Monsters: Alive and Well in 2019. J.J. Baker and Amy Lennard Goehner, copywriters. Special issue, *Life Magazine,* 2019.
Gordon, Michael D. *Scientific Babel.* London: Profile Books, 2017.
Gunerius, Ernest L. "WVTR's Sea Monster." *Radio Heritage Foundation.* https://www.radioheritage.net/Story32.asp. Retrieved 1/16/2023.
Hall, Jeffrey J. "Japan's Anti-Kaiju Fighting Force: Normalizing Japan's Self Defense Forces through Postwar Monster Films." In Mustachio and Barr, 138–160.

References

Harnisch, Larry. "June 1, 1947. Sea Monster Overpowers Troops, Destroys Tokyo! LA Men Celebrate Armed Forces Radio's 5th Anniversary with Hoax." *The Daily Mirror*, June 1, 2018. https://ladailymirror.com/2018/06/01/june-1-1947-sea-monster-overpowers-troops-destroys-tokyo-l-a-men-celebrate-armed-forces-radios-5th-anniversary-with-hoax/. Retrieved 1/17/2023.

Hillman, James. *Pan and the Nightmare*. Thompson, CT: Spring, 1972.

Hiroshi, Iwai. "Ryūjin Shinkō." *Encyclopedia of Shinto*, 2006. https://web.archive.org/web/20081203140730/http://eos.kokugakuin.ac.jp/modules/xwords/entry.php?entryID=795. Retrieved 7/29/22.

Igarashi, Yoshikuni. *Bodies of Memory: Narratives of War in Postwar Japanese Culture, 1945–1970*. Princeton: Princeton UP, 2000.

Jones, Ernest. *On the Nightmare*. London: Hogarth Press, 1912 (1920 ed.).

Jones, N.F. *Godzilla, King of the Monsters*. [Documentary.] BBC, 1988. Retrieved from http://www.youtube.com/watch?v=WdgVCn5lAKc.

Kadota, Ryūshō. *On the Brink: The Inside Story of Fukushima Daiishi*. Simon Varnam, tr. Tokyo: Kurodahan P, 2014.

Kalat, David. *A Critical History and Filmography of Toho's Godzilla Series*, 2nd Edition. Jefferson: McFarland, 2017.

Kayama, Shigeru. *Godzilla and Godzilla Raids Again*. Jeffrey Angles, tr. Minneapolis: U of Minnesota P, 2004.

Kurosawa, Akira. *Something Like an Autobiography*. Audie E. Bock, tr. New York: Vintage, 1983.

Langeland, Deirdre. *Meltdown: Earthquake, Tsunami, and Nuclear Disaster in Fukushima*. New York: Roaring Brook P, 2021.

Lanham, Url. *The Bone Hunters: The Heroic Age of Paleontology in the American West*. New York: Dover, 1973 (Kindle edition).

Lindemans, M.F. Ryujin. *Encyclopedia mythica*. Encyclopedia Mythica online, March 23, 2000 Retrieved from http://www.pantheon.org/articles/r/ryujin.html.

Lochbaum, David, Edward Lyman, Susan Q. Stranahan, and the Union of Concerned Scientists. *Fukushima: The Story of a Nuclear Disaster*. New York: New P, 2014.

McHale, Brian. *Postmodernist Fiction*. Oxford: Routledge, 1987.

Miller, R.A. *Japan's Modern Myth*. Boston: Weatherhill, 1982.

Min, Tian. "Chinese Nuo and Japanese Noh: Nuo's Role in the Origination and Formation of Noh." *Comparative Drama*, September 2003. Retrieved from https://www.thefreelibrary.com/Chinese+Nuo+and+Japanese+Noh%3a+Nuo%27s+role+in+the+origination+and...-a0120349372 (12/19/2022).

Murray, Williamson and Alan Millett. *A War to Be Won: Fighting the Second World War*. Boston: Belknap P of Harvard UP, 2000.

Mustachio, Camile D.G., and Jason Barr, eds. *Giant Creatures in Our World*. Jefferson: McFarland, 2017.

Myōjin-Shō, Kito Bayonnaise Rocks and the Sinking of the Kaiyō Maru No 5, Japan. In https://volcanohotspot.wordpress.com/2021/03/09/ō-kita-bayonnaise-rocks-and-the-sinking-of-the-kaiyo-maru-no-5-japan/comment-page-1/. Retrieved 11/22/22.

Napier, Susan. "Panic Sites: The Japanese Imagination of Disaster from *Godzilla* to *Akira*." *The Journal of Japanese Studies*, 19, no. 2 (1993): 327–351.

Noriega, C. "Godzilla and the Japanese Nightmare: When *Them!* is U.S." *Cinema Journal* 27, no. 1 (Fall 1987): 63–77.

Okuyama, Michiaki. "Religious Responses to the Atomic Bombing in Nagasaki." *Nanzan Institute for Religion and Culture* 37 (2013): 64–76.

References

O'Meara, Mallory. *The Lady from the Black Lagoon: Hollywood Monsters and the Lost Legacy of Millicent Patrick.* Toronto: Hanover Square P, 2020.
Pacific War Research Society. *The Day Man Lost.* New York: Kodansha Intl., 1972.
Petersen, D. *Invitation to Kagura: Hidden Gem of the Traditional Japanese Performing Arts.* Morrisville: Lulu Press, 2007.
Petra, Kyrie. *Godzilla Minus One [The Ultimate Movie Guide].* Kindle edition, 2023.
Petty, John E. *Stage and Scream: The Influence of Traditional Japanese Theater, Culture, and Aesthetics on Japan's Cinema of the Fantastic.* Master's Thesis. University of North Texas, May 2011.
Prince, Stephen. *The Warrior's Camera: The Cinema Art of Akira Kurosawa.* Princeton: Princeton UP, 1991.
Rankin, Andrew. *Mishima: Aesthetic Terrorist.* Honolulu: University of Hawaii P, 2018.
Rhodes, Richard. *The Making of the Atomic Bomb.* New York: Simon & Schuster, 2012.
Rhodes, Sean, and Brooke McCorkle. *Japan's Green Monsters: Environmental Commentary in Kaiju Cinema.* Jefferson: McFarland, 2018.
Roberts, Adam. *The History of Science Fiction.* London: Palgrave, 2016.
Ryfle, Steve, and Ed Godziszewski. *Ishiro Honda: A Life in Film from Godzilla to Kurosawa.* Middletown: Wesleyan UP, 2017.
"Ryujin." KCP International, 2014. Retrieved from https://www.kcpinternational.com/2014/06/the-legend-of-ryujin/ (9/12/2022).
Sadler, A.L. *Japanese Plays: Noh, Kyogen, Kabuki.* North Clarendon, VT: Tuttle, 2020. Kindle edition.
Sanders, Steven M., ed. *The Philosophy of Science Fiction Film.* Louisville: University P of Kentucky, 2008.
Shen, Sigmund C. "'Was it me? Did I kill them?' The Monsters and the Women in *King Kong* (1933), *Gojira* (1954), *Monster Zero* (1965), *Destroy all Monsters* (1968), and *Gamera III: Revenge of Iris* (1999)." In Mustachio and Barr, 92–108.
Short, Jase. "Monsters of the Rift: Kaiju as Ciphers of Unbalance." In Mustachio and Barr, 59–76.
Shumacher, M. A to Z dictionary of Japanese Buddhist Deities (1995–2013). Retrieved from http://www.onmarkproductions.com/html/tengu.shtml (8/7/22).
Skoble, Aeon J. "Technology and Ethics in *The Day the Earth Stood Still.*" In Sanders, 91–102.
Solomon, Brian. *Godzilla FAQ: All That's Left to Know about the King of the Monsters.* Lanham: Rowman & Littlefield, 2017.
Sontag, Susan. "The Imagination of Disaster." *Against Interpretation and Other Essays.* New York: Picador, 1966, 209–225.
Sorensen, Lars-Martin. *Censorship of Japanese Films During the US Occupation of Japan: the Cases of Yasujiro Ozu and Akira Kurosawa.* Lewiston, NY: Edwin Mellen P, 2009.
Spengler, Oswald. *The Decline of the West.* Charles F. Atkinson, tr. Two Volume Single Edition. New York: Cosimo Classics, 2020.
"Taiko." New World Encyclopedia. Retrieved https://www.newworldencyclopedia.org/entry/Taiko (12/9/2022).
Tanaka, Y. "Godzilla and the Bravo Shot: Who Created and Killed the Monster?" in R. Jacobs, ed., *Filling the Hole in the Nuclear Future: Art and Popular Culture Respond to the Bomb.* Lanham: Rowman & Littlefield, 2010, 159–170.
"Tomoji Abe." https://dbpedia.org/page/Tomoji_Abe. Retrieved 8/17/22.
Tsuda, Noritaki. "Human Sacrifice in Japan." *The Open Court* 12 (1918): 760–67.

References

Tsutsui, W., and M. Ito, eds. *In Godzilla's Footsteps: Japanese Pop Culture Icons on the Global Stage*. New York: Palgrave Macmillan, 2006.
Tsutsui, William. *Godzilla on My Mind*. New York: Palgrave Macmillan, 2004.
Vaz, Mark Cotta. *Living Dangerously: The Adventures of Merian C. Cooper, Creator of King Kong*. New York: Villard, 2005.
Vint, Sherryl. *Science Fiction*. Cambridge: MIT P, 2021.
Waley, Arthur. *The Noh Plays of Japan*. North Clarendon, VT: Tuttle, 1976. Kindle ed.
Wilcox, Robert K. *Japan's Secret War: How Japan's Race to Build Its Own Atomic Bomb Provided the Groundwork for North Korea's Nuclear Program*, 3rd edition. New York: Permuted P, 2019.
Wilson, William Scott, tr. and introd. *The Spirit of Noh (Fushikaden)*. Boston: Shambhala, 2006.

Index

Abe, Tomoji 7
Above and Beyond 33
Adams, Robert 123
Ahab, Captain 6–7, 87
Akasaka, Hideki 135
Akiko (adopted daughter of Noriko) 150
American Museum of Natural History 1–3, 12–13
Anderson, Mark 83
Andrews, Roy Chapman 2
Anno, Hideaki 11, 134–135
An Artist of the Floating World 19
Asahi Picture News 24
Atomic bomb program, Japanese 56–57

B-29 bomber, symbolism of 152
Bakemono (shapeshifter) 85–86
Barr, Jason 38, 103, 105
The Beast from 20,000 Fathoms 5, 32, 107, 110
Benshi 66, 69
Bikini Atoll 8
Bioluminesence 117
Black Rain 22
Blouin, Michael J. 36, 70–71, 143
Boss, Joyce E. 36, 106
Bradbury, Ray 5, 8
Bravo Shot *see* Castle Bravo
Brothers, Peter H. 67–69, 77
Bunraku 101–102; and *Gojira* puppetry 101
Burden, W. Douglas 2, 5
Burr, Raymond 15, 66

Calsbeek, Ryan 140
Campbell, Joseph 13, 15, 19, 51, 77
Carrozza, J.I. 96

Castle Bravo hydrogen bomb test 8, 72, 81
Childhood's End 71
Children of Hiroshima 24, 33
Chinkon (pacification ritual) 86
Christian history (of Japan) 94–95
Chute, Harrison 143–144
Clarke, Arthur C. 71
Conan Doyle, Arthur 66
Cooper, Merian C. 2–5
Cope, Edward Drinker 4
Cortázar, Julio 9, 123
Crossroads atomic tests 8, 148–149

Dai-Ichi Insurance Building 71
The Day the Earth Stood Still 123
deep sea trenches 113
Delgado, Marcel 4
disaster memories 137–138
Dominy, Nathaniel J. 140

Earthquake, Great East Japan (3/11) 139
Eiko Maru 40, 80
Eisenstadt, Alfred 73–74
The Emperor and the Wolf 33
Endō, Shūsaku 53

"The Fog Horn" *see* Bradbury, Ray
Foster, Michael Dylan 17, 19–20, 50, 76–77
Freedman, Carl 123, 125, 130–131
Fukushima 70, 137–138, 143; and fisheries 143
Fushikaden 11, 100

Galbraith, Stuart 33, 99
Genpatsu-shinsai (disaster theory) 141

Index

Gerow, Aaron 23
Gilmore, David D. 17
Godzilla, King of the Monsters (1956) 1, 4, 8, 66–69
Godzilla Minus One 11
Godzilla Raids Again 31
"Godzilla's egg" *see* Mishima, Yukio
Gojira: and balance 101, 111; and colonialism 125; and deleted cow scene 109, 111; and dorsal plates 117; and Emiko 39–40; as *hibakusha* 72; and Imperial lineage 88; as indigenous deity (*yuru-kayara*) 11; and intelligence 119; as Lazarus taxon 104–105; as migratory feeder 112–114; and *noh* 99–100; as *noir* 29–30; and *ōdaiko* drums 97; as *oni* 85; and radioactive breath 57, 87, 114–116; and war guilt 54
Great East Japan Earthquake 140
Great Kanto Earthquake 27

Hachiman Hill 6, 19, 52, 83
Hagiwara (reporter) 10, 40, 50–54, 59–60, 66, 108–109; as trickster figure 51
Haregushi 86
harpoon image(s) 7–8
Harryhausen, Ray 4
Hazama, Professor 134
Hibakusha 94, 135
Higuchi, Shinji 134–135
Hillman, James 18, 105
Hirada, Akihiko 152
Hirohito, Emperor 48, 77–78, 151
Hiroshima 10
Hokkaido 150
Honda, Ichiro 24–31, 34, 36, 104, 106, 150; and Buddhism 96; *Mosura* (*Mothra*) 31; and Pacific War 26–27; *Radon* (*Rodan*) 31
Honda, Kimi 6, 27, 39
Huston, John 4

Ibuse, Masuji 25
Ifukube, Akira 59, 79, 94, 134; "O Peace, O Light, Return" 59; and Shinto 96–97
Igarishi, Yoshikune 20–21, 77, 88, 101, 138

Imamura, Shohei 22
In the Shadow of Glory 99
Inada (Odo headman) 84, 109
Ishibashi, Katsuhiko 141
Ishiguro, Kazuo 19
Ishikawa, Yu 5
Iwanaga, Frank 68; as U.S. concentration camp inmate 68
Iwanaga, Tomo 68; as auxiliary *benshi* 69
Izu Archipelago (Tokyo Islands) 52, 80, 82, 112
Izu-Bonin Trench 113–114
Izuma 52, 65, 81–84, 86, 89–90, 108–110; and Ryuja 83

Japanese geology 120–121
Jimmu 87
Jones, Ernest 17–18
Jurassic Park 109, 116

Kachidoki Bridge 119
Kagura ceremony 86
Kaiyō Maru Number Five 80
Kalat, David 54, 109, 114
Kamakura-san 140
Kamata-kun 140
Kan, Prime Minister Naoto 141
Kayama, Shigeru 5, 7, 22–23, 37, 41, 106; revised Gojira novel of 1955 22–23
King Kong 4, 90
Knight, Charles R, paintings of 3–4
Kochi, Momoko 7
Kôdô, Kokuten 89
Kojiki 11, 83, 90
Komodo dragons 2–3, 5
Kowairo setsumi 67
Kuniyoshi, Utagawa 83
Kurosawa, Akira 25–27, 148; *The Bad Sleep Well* 31; *Do-des-ka-den* 28, 148; *High and Low* 31; *Ikiru* 25, 148; *Madadayo* 28, 148; *The Men Who Tread on the Tiger's Tail* 27; *No Regrets for Our Youth* 38; *One Wonderful Sunday* 28–29, 148; *Ran* 28, 31; *Record of a Living Being (I Live in Fear)* 25–26, 31–35, 60, 73; *Rhapsody in August* 28, 31; *Seven Samurai* 25, 34–35, 99; *Stray Dog* 27, 35, 148
Kurosawa, Heigo 27

164

Index

Langeland, Deirdre 137–138, 141
Lem, Stanisław 122–124
Lochbaum, David 140, 142–143
The Lost World 66
Lucky Dragon Five 71, 81, 93; and Eiko-Maru 81
Lukács, Georg 124, 131

MacArthur, Douglas 21, 48, 71, 78, 150
Maki, Goro 134–135, 138
Malone, Ed 66
Marsh, Othniel 4
Marshall Islands 113
Martin, Steve (character) 15, 61, 66–69, 72, 129
Masaji 52
McHale, Brian 122; and the dominant 122
Mifune, Toshiro 26
Min, Tian 102
Mishima, Yukio 10, 36, 78
Misogi-no-kokyu-ho (ritual of the breath) 87; and oxygen destroyer 87
Moby Dick 4, 7–8, 113
monster hoax (1947) 21–22, 150
Morse, Terry 66–67, 129
Murata, Takeo 42
Myōjin-shō (volcano) 80, 121

Nagasaki 10
Nakajima, Haruo 26, 100, 102
Nihon Shoki 11, 51, 65, 87, 89, 145
Ningen Sengen (Humanity Declaration) 48, 77–78
Nishina, Yushio 57
Noda, Kenji 148, 151, 152; and Akihiko Hirata 152
Noh, influence of 96–97; types of 98
Noriega, Chon 34
nuclear event 74

O'Brien, Willis 4, 22
Occupation of Japan, Allied 18, 24, 33–36, 39, 76, 78, 89, 150
Odo Island 6, 19–20, 41, 52, 79–82, 97, 108, 149; location of 52, 79–80; and *sakoku* Japan 91–92; and Shinto 97
Ogashira, Hiromi 140, 142
Ogata, Hideto 7, 10, 18, 27–29, 39–47, 61–63

Oishi, Noriko 149; and Emiko Yamane 150
Okochi, Prime Minister 144
Omiai/Ren'a 62; as Go arrangements 40
Oni (evil spirit) 85, 102; masks and Gojira's countenance 102
Operation Meetinghouse 39
Osborn, Henry Fairfield 2
oxygen destroyer 9, 19, 50, 64, 73–75; as byproduct of atomic program 54–57, 73; as contradiction of Shinto breath principles 87

Pikadon (atomic fireball) 73
Purojekuto G-Sakuhin 22

Reyes, Aldana 127–129, 137
RIKEN 56–57
Ryfle, Steve 39
Ryfle and Godziszewski 29
Ryuja (Messenger of Ryujin) 83
Ryujin 83–84, 86; in folktales 83–84; as Gojira precursor 83; as imperial ancestor 87–88
Ryujin Shinko 84, 92; as *kagura* ceremony 84

Sadler, A.J. 96
Sagami Trench 114
Sagisu, Shirō 134
Sakai, Sachio 51
Sakhalin 150
Sakoku 94–95
Sasaki, Sadako 134
The Sea and Poison 53
Sekigawa, Hideo 33
Serizawa, Daisuke 7, 15, 27, 29, 46–54, 59–60, 63–64, 74–75; and battle with Ogata over oxygen destroyer 46, 50–51; and German affiliations 53–54, 59; and Ian Malcolm 75; isolation of 46–47; representation of age 47–48; and J. Robert Oppenheimer 75; and suicide 48–50, 60, 64, 78; as *yōkai taiji* (monster slayer) 51
Shide 86
Shikishima, Kōichi 147, 149–150, 152; and Serizawa 149, 153
Shimenawa, ritual protective cords 86, 92

165

Index

Shimura, Takashi 26, 37
Shin Godzilla 11, 70
Shinagawa-kun 140
Shinagawa rail yards 10, 41
Shinden J7W (interceptor) 152
Shinkichi 10, 52, 63; as *kokata* 98
Shomin geki 28–29
Short, Jase 25, 82
Sikorski H-19 (helicopter) 80
Sontag, Susan 73
Sorensen, Lars-Martin (*Censorship of Japanese Films*) 34
Stalin, Josef 150
Sueto, Ito see *Children of Hiroshima*
Suitmation 99, 101
Sukiyabashi bridge 39, 129
Sundas, Lesser 2
Susano (*Susan'oo, Su-san-oo*) 51, 145
Suvin, Darko 126

Tachibana, Sosaku 152
Tachibana-hime 89
Tailieiki 90
Taisho period 61
Takao, IJN 149, 151
Takarada, Akira 115
Tanabe, Professor 33, 41, 43, 72, 93
Tanaka, Tomoyuki 5–6, 21, 28, 99
TEPCO 140–141, 145–146
Toho Studios 22, 91
Tokaimura crisis 142
Tomai, Masao (cinematographer) 119
Treaty of San Francisco 24
Tsuburaya, Eiji 17, 22, 30–31, 85–86, 96, 98
Tsuda, Noritaki 65, 89–91
Tsutsui, William 13, 35, 71
20,000 Leagues Under the Sea 5

Ujigami 82
Ukiyo-e 83
Uranium Hexafluoride 57

Ward, Al C. 9
What Is Your Name? (*Kimi no Na wa*) 39, 129

Yaguchi, Rando 134–135, 138, 144–145
Yamabushi tengu 86–87
Yamada, Koji see Kayama, Shigero
Yamane, Emiko 7, 15, 18–19, 27–29, 37–41, 43, 50, 61, 63, 90, 152–153; and Ann Darrow 90; as Benten, goddess of compassion 64, 91; as Princess Tamatori 83
Yamane, Professor Kyohei 10, 19–20, 29, 37, 40–43, 61, 72, 74, 83, 89, 93, 104–107, 132, 135–136, 152; moral transformation 42–43
Yamata no Orochi 51
Yamatodamashii 79
Yamazaki, Takashi 11, 21fn., 147; *Always: Sunset on Third Street* 147–148; *The Eternal Zero* 21fn., 147, 149; *The Great War of Archimedes* 21fn., 147–149
Yanigata kunio school of folklore 83–84
Yōgō Pine (on Noh stage) 102–103; and mushroom cloud 102–103
Yokai 17, 77, 149
Yokoyama, Matajiro 37
Yoshida, Masao 139fn, 141, 143, 145
Yoshioka, Hidetaka (as Noda) 148
Yoshiori, Project 135, 145
Yukie see *No Regrets for Our Youth*

Zeami 11, 100; and Nakajima's performance 100
Zhili-Fengtian conflict 2

www.ingramcontent.com/pod-product-compliance
Lightning Source LLC
Chambersburg PA
CBHW032048300426
44117CB00009B/1229